NEW LIFE FOR THE WALKING DEAD

Oliver E. Rogers

WestBow Press books may be ordered through booksellers or by contacting:

WestBow Press
A Division of Thomas Nelson & Zondervan
1663 Liberty Drive
Bloomington, IN 47403
www.westbowpress.com
1 (866) 928-1240

ISBN: 978-1-9736-3005-0 (sc)
ISBN: 978-1-9736-3006-7 (hc)
ISBN: 978-1-9736-3007-4 (e)

Library of Congress Control Number: 2018906659

Print information available on the last page.

WestBow Press rev. date: 06/22/2018

Endorsements

It is refreshing to read a book where the author has a heart for Jesus, for heaven and for helping others find their way to both. Oliver Rogers is a man of the Word and writes in a simple, straight forward manner so only those who refuse the simple teachings of scripture may be inclined to disagree.

Demonstrating great perception on familiar texts, Oliver has an in-depth biblical understanding of the church and what we should look like today. Ending with a plea that "Unity is Possible," Oliver draws readers back to the Word and challenges each of us to be obedient followers.

Louis F. Butterfield
Ed. D., Professor Emeritus
Harding University, Searcy, Arkansas

"The Mission of Jesus Christ," by Oliver Rogers, is a must read and study for every student of the Bible. Rogers provides an excellent panoramic overview of Christ's mission here upon the earth, and he masterly develops the interwoven relationship between the "Kingdom" and the "Church."

Rogers concludes with Christ's prayer for unity and encourages us to strive for this goal by applying the principles of the Golden Rule.

Toney M. Bucchi
Vice Admiral, retired
United States Navy
tbucchi@harding.edu

Oliver Rogers has reached into his decade of study to summarize the high points of the themes of the New Testament. It is difficult if not impossible to think of any major topic he has left untouched. The book is both a great doorway into New Testament studies for the novice and an insightful review for the long-time Christian.

Gayle Crowe
Doctor of Ministry
V.P. of Programing

World Christian Broadcasting

Dedication

To my children, Carolyn, Marilyn, Melanie and Sherman who have been very supportive of my ministry from the time they were old enough to sit and listen to a lesson until this book was complete.

We have always been a close family. The children have enjoyed coming home to spend time with mom and dad. It's true, they have their own families to care for and support, but mom and dad are precious to them and this provides great satisfaction and comfort to us.

I love them dearly and want them to be there "when the role is called up yonder."

Dad, Oliver

Acknowledgments

Two people who have devoted hours to reading this manuscript are my sister, Dorma Rainey, and her husband, Dr. Gene Rainey. Dorma was looking at sentence structure while checking for grammatical errors. Gene focused on content and arrangement of materials. Both are excellent students of the Scriptures. Their contribution is greatly appreciated.

Dr. C. Philip Slate, who has written the *Foreword,* has critiqued the book with care and offered a number of very helpful suggestions. His insightful thoughts have helped me to give greater attention to emphasizing the spiritual change essential to living the abundant life that Jesus promised his followers. His thoughts are greatly appreciated.

The final reading has been done by my wife, Norma. Her evaluation is very important because she, unlike others, is courageous enough to tell me when something needs to be changed, stated in a better way or left out. I pay careful attention to her suggestions because she is generally right. Thank you Norma.

To all of these I express my sincere appreciation for their efforts to help make the final draft a better book.

Contents

Foreword

People are often prone to make the Christian way seem simpler than it really is. Dr. James D. Bales once told about a friend of his who typed the text of John 3:16 on a card and stuck it to a wooden post in his warehouse, declaring, "Bales, there is my Bible!" Bales quipped, "It's a little one, isn't it?" Of course, Scripture has the quality to appeal to both young and old, to the simple and the brilliant. Gregory the Great once commented that Scripture is like a stream in which the lamb may wade and the elephant swim. Both experience are valid, but there are great advantages in seeing the Christian way in its broader biblical context. Numerous biblical concepts and institutions are best understood and best appreciated when they are viewed in the overall context of Scripture.

In the 19th century Robert Milligan wrote the useful work, *The Scheme of Redemption,* in which he used the entire biblical story-line as the context for understanding salvation. More recently, Everett Ferguson produced the helpful work, *The Church of Christ: a biblical theology for today,* in which he placed "the church" or "the people of God" in the broader context of the biblical story-line. As the title indicates, Oliver Rogers' book deals chiefly with the mission and ministry of Jesus, with special reference to the reign of God. The thrust of Jesus' work, however, is seen more poignantly against the broader background of the Old Testament themes of the kingdom of God. It is a good, mid-level presentation of the antecedents of the reign of God and the Christian response under the new covenant.

Toward the end of the book Rogers stresses the importance of unity among people who sincerely and seriously seek to follow Jesus, to live under the reign of God. This is a word in season. The modern ecumenical movement that began in the early 20th century had its roots in the non-Western mission fields. Missionary efforts were hindered by the multiplicity of churches with strange names and bickering leaders. An entire century of thought, meetings, and writings on unity, however, has revealed some great divides among the broader Christian world. Rogers does not seek to appeal to those big divides, like Roman Catholicism, Orthodoxy, and Reformed churches. His appeal is more to those who hold a high view of Scripture; and his appeal is timely since, especially in North America, many people who still want to say "Yes" to Jesus are saying "No" to the churches they know. The literature on the "Nones" is quite large and growing. By "nones" I mean those who may regard themselves as Christians or "spiritual" who pray and read Scripture, but who when asked about their church affiliation check "None." They perceive the churches with which they are familiar as shallow and unrelated to their positions, failing to answer convincingly and substantively many of their basic questions of life. It is easy to castigate that shallowness, but Rogers desires to take a higher road and make a positive appeal for people to follow the essentials, throw away the trivial, and strive together to honor God in his world.

This book comes from many years of ministry from among a diverse group of people from and within the context of a local church. Rogers is one of those thoughtful preachers who combine studiousness with warm application to the human situation. His book will serve well those who want to move beyond their necessarily elementary beginning in Christ. Fowler and others have pointed out various stages of faith development, and while it takes more than intellectual activity to grow, deepening one's understanding of the Christian's place in the story-line of Scripture can make a notable contribution to faith development. I commend this book as a helpful mid-level treatment of one of the great themes of Scripture, the rule of God in human life.

—C. Philip Slate. Retired professor, author of *Missions Handbook for Local Churches, Lest We Forget: Mini-biographies of Missionaries of a Bygone Generation, and (with* Stan Granberg) *Reaching 'Russia'.*

Introduction

These are critical and troubled times for people of every age. Thousands of our bright young teens and adults are dying as a result of overdosing on opioid drugs. Why? They have no sense of purpose for living and are unable to find peace and comfort. Think of the misery and anguish this is causing their family!

This *book* provides answers to questions that offer a genuine sense of purpose for why we are living. They are: *Where did I come from? Why am I here? Is there life after death? If so, where? How can I know if or where I will live eternally after I die? What must I do to get forgiveness of my sins? Does God really care about me?*

Jesus Christ came down from heaven and lived as a human being for a little more than 33 years. Think of it—he did more to change the course of history and the true meaning of life than all of the great intellectuals combined! He said, "I came that they may have life, and have it more abundantly" (John 10:10, Confraternity).

The apostle John wrote that Jesus did many more miracles while with his disciples than the ones recorded in his gospel, but the ones included had *one purpose,* to convince the reader that Jesus was who he claimed to be, "the Christ, the Son of God" (John 20:30-31). Jesus stated emphatically: "I am the way and the truth and the life. No one comes to the Father except through me" (John 14:6).

His ministry frequently provided an opportunity to perform miracles. For example, *he turned water to wine* at a wedding feast in Cana of Galilee when the wine ran out; *he fed 5000 people from the little boy's lunch* consisting of five loaves and two fish; *he walked on water* while going to his disciples who were in the boat; he *opened the eyes of a man who was born blind; he raised dead Lazarus who had been in the grave four days;* and there is more. His miracles provided evidence of his *supernatural power* and authority.

Unless and until we come to know God through a personal relationship with Jesus Christ, we are all walking around dead in our sins. (Ephesians 2:1-10). Examples are included in the *book* explaining what we must do to receive forgiveness of our sins, and ultimately eternal life in heaven.

Are you just another of today's living dead, trudging through the muck and mire of a joyless, meaningless existence? You can break that cycle! Here's how you can be lifted up through the life, death and resurrection of Jesus Christ.

What are you apart from God but a spiritual zombie, a member of the walking dead who doesn't even realize that you are dead? Discover the transcendent, freeing power in the universe. It's the love of God. You can have it and it won't break the bank.

The story doesn't end here but continues with Jesus explaining that he was going away to prepare a place for his people (John14:1-11).

Luke, the physician, was given the honor of recording the account of Jesus telling his disciples they were to be his witnesses in Jerusalem, Judea, Samaria, and to the ends of the earth. "After he said this, he was taken up before their very eyes, and a cloud hid him from their sight" (Acts 1:9). Suddenly, two men dressed in white asked: why are you standing here looking into the sky? This same Jesus who has gone to heaven will return in the same way you have seen him go into heaven (vv. 10, 11).

The following Pentecost miraculous events began to take place that required help from the apostle Peter for the people to understand. A complete explanation is given in Acts chapter 2, including the beginning of the kingdom and the church. The sudden growth created division between the Jewish leaders and the apostles. Churches began to spring up so rapidly that the Jewish leaders felt compelled to take action against the apostles. They arrested Peter and John and had them put in jail. From this point, Judaism begins to decline and Christianity flourishes.

This is where the Lord chose Saul of Tarsus, soon to be known as Paul, the apostle of Christ Jesus. (Acts 26:15-18). Under his leadership, Christianity spread rapidly throughout the entire Roman world. The Lord's commission was then and is now:

> Therefore go and make disciples of all nations, baptizing them in the name of the Father and of the Son and of the Holy Spirit, and teaching them to obey everything I have commanded you. And surely I am with you always, to the very end of the age (Matthew 28:19, 20).
>
> He is coming back to take us home to heaven. Will you be ready?

Section One

The Mission of Jesus Christ

Who Then Can Be Saved?

"A certain ruler asked...' Good teacher, what must I do to inherit eternal life?" "Why do you call me good?' 'Jesus answered.'

"No one is Good—except God alone." (Luke 18:18,19).

"Those who heard this asked," "Who then can be saved?" (v-26)

"Jesus replied, "What is impossible with men is possible with God" (Luke 18:27).

Chapter 1

God's Eternal Plan Completed in Jesus

> *For what will a man be profited, if he gains the whole world, and forfeits his soul? Or what will a man give in exchange for his soul? (Matthew 16:26)*[1]

Every thing written from this comment forward has purpose only in light of what Jesus Christ stated in this passage. If we are living only for what can be gained from this life, then Solomon's message in Ecclesiastes 2:10, 11, is most appropriate:

> I denied myself nothing my eyes desired;
> I refused myself no pleasure.
> My heart took delight in all my work,
> And this was the reward of all my labor.
> Yet when I surveyed all that my hands had done,
> and what I had toiled to achieve,
> everything was meaningless,
> a chasing after the wind;
> nothing was gained under the sun.

Solomon was reminding us that if our life consists of nothing more than what we *gain* or add to our bank account today; if there is nothing more to life than what is experienced here, then is it really worth the effort? Jesus offers us a better life than all of the world's wealth gained under the sun.

My sincere desire is that as you continue to read, the words of Jesus in the above quotation will keep returning to your mind and make an impression that cannot be erased. I hope you will keep reading until you reach the grand finale in the last chapter where you will find that joyful refrain, "Well done, good and faithful servant: enter into the joy of your Lord" where eternal life in heaven will be your final reward (Matthew 25:21-23). This statement provides true meaning to the mission of Jesus as he began his ministry regarding the kingdom of heaven.

Background Information to the Mission of Jesus Christ

In reading the Scriptures, we find the first word recorded that Jesus spoke to begin his public ministry was "*Repent*" (Matthew 4:17). That was followed by the expression, "for the kingdom of heaven is near." Could the Lord have chosen a more subtle term that would have been less offensive to his audience, and still would have achieved the same results? Jesus knew that only very strong language would touch the people's hearts and cause them to turn away from their sinful practices. Therefore, our Savior did not waste time getting to the message that would appeal to their hearts and minds and turn them back to God.

The need for repentance and the introduction of the kingdom are both matters essential to our salvation and will be examined farther along in this study.

In reflecting on the world of the first century and the method Jesus used to get the people's attention, I am reminded of what a family member recently shared while discussing conditions in today's society. She commented regarding how precious little so-called

Christians are doing today to reach people living in sin without God in their lives. The truth is that the majority of the religious world has become lethargic—fallen asleep—and needs a wakeup call!

Recent surveys reveal that 40% of the American public are "unchurched." By 2050, the figure is projected to rise to 50% of Americans who will remain home on Sunday mornings. The US citizens are rapidly becoming secularized and religiously uncommitted. In effect, the American nation is moving toward the same condition of European nations, such as England where almost 90% of the population is "unchurched."

It is my sincere hope that throughout this study thoughts are being introduced that will help to bring Christians together. We'll be motivated to use every legitimate means available to reach people around us who are drowning in sin and will face the judgment unprepared to meet God if they are not rescued.

God Has Reigned from the Beginning of Creation

The God who created this universe and every living thing that exists within it, is presented in Scripture as a loving, compassionate, merciful heavenly Father. The point at which He created the first two human beings, Adam and Eve, His intent was for them to live forever and produce offspring. All went well until they made the wrong choice and disobeyed their Creator. This decision led to their separation from God and resulted in sin and death coming into their lives.

Generations were allowed to come and go before God was ready to reconcile the human race to Himself through the person of Jesus Christ.

Humanity Became Exceedingly Wicked

As the human race multiplied and was given oversight of the creation, people began to turn away from God and become extremely wicked. This development displeased the Creator to the point that He was ready to wipe the human race from the earth. Had it not been for righteous Noah and his family, the flood would have brought an end to the human family (Genesis 6:9-22). Following the flood, the process of restoring and rebuilding all that was destroyed by the flood took generations.

Later, God chose Abram, whose name was changed to Abraham, by whose descendants all the families of the earth were to be blessed (Genesis 12:1-3). As Abraham's family multiplied and grew into the nation of Israel, judges were selected to give direction to the different tribes and families and to rule over them. The judges, a type of political system, was practiced for a number of generations until Samuel the prophet appeared.

The People's Desire for a King to Be Their Ruler

During the rule of Samuel's two wicked sons, Joel and Abijah, the people became restless and insisted on having a king to rule over them (1 Samuel 8:4-7). The prophet prayed to the Lord for guidance but was surprised by the answer he received. God declared: "Listen to all that the people are saying to you; it is not you they have rejected, but they have rejected me as their king" (8:7). Please note: God declared that the people had rejected HIM from being king over them.

Following the Lord's command, Samuel appointed Saul, the son of Kish, as the first king to rule the nation of Israel. Early in his reign, Saul ruled in a satisfactory manner, but in time he disobeyed the Lord and was removed from the kingdom. He was killed in battle against the Philistines, as was his son, Jonathan, who as the royal prince was next in line to ascend the throne (1 Samuel 31:1-6). Saul was succeeded in the kingdom by David, the son of Jesse, who is referred to as "a man after My (God's) heart who will do all My will" (Acts 13:22, NASV). David and his son, Solomon, were kings over a united Israel, which was a nation of power and prestige because it was blessed by God (1 Samuel 9:12).

Solomon reigned in Jerusalem over all Israel for forty years. Early in the young king's reign, he was careful to rule in a manner that pleased God and his leadership was blessed abundantly. With the passing of time, Solomon became too involved with women and turned to worshipping idols. The record states that "He had 700 wives of royal birth, and 300 concubines and his wives led him astray" (1 Kings 11:3). The Lord became angry with Solomon because he did evil and his heart was not fully devoted to God.

One is left to wonder if both David and Solomon were familiar with the Lord's instruction regarding marriage since both men had several wives. Had polygamy become such a common practice that they simply ignored the teaching?

- ✓ Jewish history from Solomon's death until the conclusion of the exiles is a violent record of frequent warfare between the Southern and Northern kingdoms. The majority of the kings who ruled over the Northern kingdom were described as doing evil in the eyes of the Lord, walking in the ways of their fathers (1Kings 15:26).

God warned the inhabitants of both Israel and Judah through the prophets and seers to avoid idol worship. "But they would not listen, and were as stiff-necked as their fathers who did not trust in the Lord their God" (2 Kings 17:14). This behavior resulted in the Lord rejecting the people of Israel and allowing them to be taken into captivity in Assyria (vv. 18-23).

The rulers of the Southern Kingdom— Judah— made a greater effort to maintain peace than did Israel. Unlike the kings of the north, they were careful to do good and right in the eyes of the Lord and to walk in the ways of their father, David. This last statement is repeated several times, indicating that the way David lived generally was pleasing to the Lord.

When Hezekiah was king of Judah, Sennacherib, king of Assyria, brought a mighty army against Jerusalem to destroy the city. The

Lord sent a message to Hezekiah by Isaiah, the prophet, saying: "I will defend this city and save it for my sake and for *the sake of David my servant"* (2 Kings 19:34, emphasis added). Because of Hezekiah's faithfulness and prayers. God sent an angel of the Lord to destroy 185,000 men of the Assyrian army. As a result, Sennacherib broke camp quickly and returned to Nineveh (2 Kings 19).

Josiah is the last king in Judah to be commended highly. He became king at the age of eight and reigned in Jerusalem fifty-five years. During his reign, the Book of the Law was found in the Temple. After it was read in the presence of the king, Josiah arranged to have its decrees followed completely. This decision called for total destruction of all the idolatrous practices that had been introduced since the days of Solomon. He "got rid of the mediums and spiritists, the household gods, the idols and all the other detestable things seen in Judah and Jerusalem" (2 Kings 23:24). His achievements are summarized with these words:

Neither before nor after Josiah was there a king like him who turned to the Lord as he did—with all his heart and with all his soul and with all his strength, in accordance with all the Law of Moses (v.25).

It is sad, but true, that every king in Judah following Josiah did evil in the eyes of the Lord. The story ends as follows: "So all Judah went into captivity, away from their land" (2 Kings 25:21b).

Things Necessary for a Kingdom to Exist

Four requirements are necessary for a kingdom to exist:

- ☑ First, a person must assume the role of king.
- ☑ Second, there must be a territory over which the king rules.
- ☑ Third, there must be subjects or citizens, who live within the territory.
- ☑ Fourth, a legal system is required for a king to govern his citizens.

These four requirements apply to every kingdom—whether physical or spiritual.

The Prophecy of Daniel

Centuries before Jesus came peaching, "Repent, for the kingdom of heaven is near," the prophet Daniel prophesied about this kingdom that God would establish. He foretold that four earthly kingdoms would rise and fall before the beginning of a kingdom established by the God of heaven. That kingdom Daniel declared, "will never be destroyed, and that kingdom...will crush and put an end to all these kingdoms, but it will itself endure forever" (Daniel 2:44).

> Daniel's prophecy was spoken to Nebuchadnezzar, king of Babylon, who had a dream that confused and troubled him. He summoned the wise men, magicians, conjurers and diviners to interpret the dream, but he refused to relate the dream's contents to them. Because they could not tell the king the contents and interpretation of the dream, Nebuchadnezzar was "furious and gave orders to destroy all the wise men of Babylon" (Daniel 2:12).

The prophet came to the rescue of the condemned men and convinced the king that the God of heaven would give him an answer. Arioch, the king's attendant, took Daniel before the king. When asked if he could make known the dream and its interpretation, Daniel replied:

> As for the mystery about which the king has inquired, neither wise men, conjurers, magicians, nor diviners are able to declare it to the king. However, there is a God in heaven who reveals mysteries, and *He has made known to King Nebuchadnezzar what will take place in the latter days.* This was your dream and the visions in your mind while on your bed (Daniel 2:27-28, NASV, emphasis added).

At that point, Daniel explained the dream and its interpretation, which included four kingdoms.

- ☑ First kingdom: Babylonian empire, over which Nebuchadnezzar reigned.
- ☑ Second kingdom: Medes and Persians.
- ☑ Third kingdom: Alexandrian Empire.
- ☑ Fourth kingdom: Roman Empire.

Numerous details of these empires are found in Daniel 2:36-43. Beginning with verse 44, the prophet explained that,

> "in the days of those kings the God of heaven will set up a kingdom which will never be destroyed, and that kingdom will not be left for another people; it will crush and put an end to all these kingdoms, but it will itself endure forever."

This prophecy of an everlasting, divinely established kingdom was fulfilled by Jesus when he said: "Repent for the kingdom of heaven is near" (Matthew 4:17). It is the same kingdom Luke wrote about in Acts chapter two that had its beginning in A.D.33 on the Day of Pentecost in the city of Jerusalem.

On a later occasion Daniel interpreted another of King Nebuchadnezzar's dreams, informing him that he would be driven away from people and would live with the wild animals "until you acknowledge that the Most High is sovereign over the kingdoms of men and gives them to anyone he wishes" (4:32).

These introductory thoughts set the stage for the coming of the Messiah, Jesus Christ, into the world. His purpose was to rescue the human race from sin and condemnation while preparing us for the new and abundant life in Christ here and for eternity.

Summary

God reigned over the nations who functioned as a kingdom centuries before the nation of Israel came into existence. For generations, the people became exceedingly wicked.

Had it not been for righteous Noah, and his family, the Lord would have wiped the human race from the face of the earth.

Much later, God chose a man named Abraham through whom he planned to raise up a nation called Israel.

As the people of Israel multiplied, they insisted on being ruled by a king like the nations around them. The prophet Samuel prayed to God for an answer and was told to let them have a king because they had not rejected the prophet, but the Lord Himself.

Later, the prophet, Daniel, spoke about a kingdom to Nebuchadnezzar, the king of Babylon, that in time the God of heaven would set up that would never be destroyed.

The point at which Jesus began his ministry, he spoke of this kingdom as being nearby.

Chapter two examines the birth, childhood and temptation of Jesus by Satan.

Jesus Was Born to the Virgin Mary

The Angel: "You will be with child and give birth to a son, And you are to give him the name Jesus" (Luke 1:31). Mary: "How Will this be,... since I am a virgin?" (v.34)

"What is impossible with man, is possible with God" (v.37).

Chapter 2

Unique Events Regarding Jesus Christ

Two events in the life of Jesus Christ stand out above all the rest: his birth and his resurrection. Numerous accounts that fill the pages between these miraculous happenings serve to support and reinforce the truth of Jesus' birth and resurrection.

Expectations of the Messiah

Generations of Jewish people were convinced from Old Testament teaching that God would, in time, send the Messiah who would serve as their deliverer from captivity by the enemy and usher in a glorious age of eternal bliss.

Moses referred to the time when God would raise up a prophet like himself with the following thought:

> The Lord your God will raise up for you a prophet like me from among your brothers. You must listen to him.... I will put my words in his mouth, and he will tell them everything I command him. If anyone does not listen to my words that the prophet

> speaks in my name, I myself will call him to account (Deuteronomy 18:15, 18, 19).

We know that this prophecy is about Jesus Christ because the apostle Peter included it in his statement regarding, "how God fulfilled what he had foretold through all the prophets saying that his Christ would suffer" (Acts 3:18 and 22, 23). Peter quoted the prophecy of Moses and declared emphatically that it was referring to Jesus Christ.

The prophet, Isaiah, writing in the seventh century B. C., mentioned how the Lord would give them a sign:

> "Therefore the Lord himself will give you a sign. The virgin will be with child and will give birth to a son, and will call him Immanuel" (Isaiah 7:14).

Matthew, wrote about the birth of Jesus, uses the above quotation and explained that *Immanuel* means, "God with us" (Matthew 1:23).

The prophet Micah wrote about one who would come from Bethlehem to rule over Israel:

> But you Bethlehem Ephrathah, though you are small among the clans of Judah, out of you will come for me one who will be ruler over Israel, whose origins are from old, from ancient times (Micah 5:2). Matthew quoted from this passage in (2:6).

For generations the Israelite people lived expecting the Messiah to come. However, when Jesus did appear, the religious leaders' understanding of how and where he would make his appearance had little in common with their expectations. The same was true of what he would do and teach. Consequently, their rejection was voiced quickly and with no uncertainty.

From the beginning, the religious leaders had a problem regarding Jesus' birth: he was considered to be an illegitimate child. When

Mary reported that she was with child, Joseph knew that he was not the father. He decided to call off the wedding quietly rather than to expose Mary to public disgrace.

In time, the story was circulated among family and friends that an angel had appeared to Joseph and Mary, assuring them that Mary, a virgin, would conceive and bear a son by means of the Holy Spirit. Little wonder that the religious leaders had difficulty accepting the validity of this story. The reality was that Mary was the only person who could speak with certainty regarding her virginity.

An additional problem: Joseph and Mary were common, ordinary people from the city of Nazareth in Galilee. To the religious Pharisees and Sadducees, Jesus made his entrance through the wrong territory—Nazareth of Galilee. In addition, the people who accompanied him were ordinary fishermen. Couple these events with the people he befriended—lepers, adulterers, despised tax collectors—and the result was more than the religious Pharisees and Sadducees could stomach. They expected him to be ushered in through an intelligent, religious Pharisee family.

A Look At Jesus' Birth

Matthew begins the account of Jesus' birth in this way:

> This is how the birth of Jesus Christ came about. His mother Mary was pledged to be married to Joseph, but before they came together, she was found to be with child through the Holy Spirit. Because Joseph her husband was a righteous man and did not want to expose her to public disgrace, he had in mind to divorce her quietly (Matthew 1:18, 19).

Faced with similar circumstances, what would you have done? Everything you have known about this young woman causes you to believe that she was an honest, sincere, and truthful young lady. It is obvious now that she is with child. All the time you have spent together you know that sexual relations have not taken place. Mary declares she has not had relations with any man; so what are you to believe and do? As a righteous person, after great reflection, you decide to end the relationship quietly rather than expose her to public disgrace. You have never faced a public decision of this magnitude. Undoubtedly, thoughts such as these were racing through Joseph's mind as he wrestled with what he should do.

Then Joseph had a strange dream: the Lord appeared to him, explaining that he was not to hesitate or be fearful "to take Mary home as your wife, because what is conceived in her is from the Holy Spirit" (Matthew 1:12). Mary was to give birth to a son who would be named Jesus, which means "Savior." Do you suppose Joseph was wondering if his mind through a dream was playing tricks on him?

Joseph was familiar with Isaiah's prophecy that a virgin would conceive and bear a child, who would be called "Immanuel," meaning "God with us" (Matthew 1:23). Once he awoke, he followed the angel's instructions and took Mary to become his wife. They had no sexual relations until after the child was born.

What can be stated with certainty regarding this event?

- Joseph and Mary were planning to get married.
- One day Mary announces to Joseph that she is pregnant.
- Mary knows that she has not had sexual relations with any man.
- Joseph is aware that they have not engaged in sex.

Fortunately, Joseph was a devoutly religious person, acquainted with Old Testament Scripture. He had no hesitation in believing that an angel had delivered the dream to him. Matthew gives a sketchy account of these events, but simply concludes that when Joseph awoke, he obeyed the Lord's command, "and took Mary home as his wife. But he had no union with her until she gave birth to a son. And he gave him the name Jesus" (Matthew 1:24, 25).

As for Mary, the angel appeared to her and announced that she would be "with child and give birth to a son who would be given the name Jesus" (Luke 1:31). This announcement was shocking to Mary because she was a virgin who had never been intimate with any man. We can only imagine her relief when the angel declared, "The Holy Spirit will come upon you, and the power of the Most High will overshadow you. So the holy one to be born will be called the Son of God" (Luke 1:35). Suddenly, the entire account begins to make sense. Mary now understands why the angel said that she had "found favor with God" (v. 30). Never again would there be doubt in her mind regarding the child's origin. From that day forward, it was absolutely certain to both Joseph and Mary that the birth of Jesus Christ truly was miraculous since he was conceived by the Holy Spirit.

Luke Offers More Details about Jesus' Birth

Luke records the birth account in greater detail and explains why Joseph and Mary made the trip to Bethlehem where Jesus was born. Caesar Augustus had issued a decree declaring that a census must be taken of the entire Roman world and that everyone was required to register in his hometown. The account included that Jesus' first baby bed was a wooden trough used to feed the animals (Luke 2). He explained how shepherds were informed by an angel regarding the child's birth with the message:

> I bring you good news of great joy that will be for all the people. Today in the town of David a Savior has been born to you; he is Christ the Lord: (Luke 2:10,11).

Matthew records the visit of the Magi (wise men), who saw his star in the east and came to Bethlehem, asking: "Where is the one who has been born king of the Jews?" (2:2) The star continued to guide them until they arrived at the house where the child and Mary were staying. They were no longer sharing the facilities where livestock were kept but had been moved into a house (Matthew 2:11).

Early Childhood of Jesus

Little is recorded regarding the childhood years of Jesus. Following the visit of the magi, an angel of the Lord appeared to Joseph in a dream, telling him to take the child and his mother and escape to Egypt because King Herod intended to kill him. After Herod died, the angel instructed Joseph to take his family and return to Nazareth in Galilee. Luke explains that while they lived in Galilee, Jesus grew and was obedient to his parents.

The Temple Episode

Luke relates an interesting account of the Lord when he was twelve years old. His parents had taken him to Jerusalem for the yearly Feast of the Passover, an event that was never missed by the family. Once the Passover event was completed, the parents began their journey home, not realizing that Jesus had remained behind in Jerusalem. At the end of the day, they began looking for him among relatives and friends. Since he was nowhere to be found, they hastily returned to Jerusalem to look for him. It took three days before he was located "in the temple courts, sitting among the teachers, listening to them and asking them questions" Luke 2:46). His understanding and answers amazed all who were listening.

His parents were astonished, and as expected, his mother was very disappointed at his negligent behavior. His response truly was amazing! "Why were you searching for me?" "Didn't you know that I had to be in my Father's house?" (Luke 2:49) Other versions translate:

"about my Father's business." At the time, the significance of this comment was not clear to them; nevertheless, they returned home to Nazareth where he was obedient to them. Mary continued to treasure these thoughts in her heart, indicating that more was implied than was understood. We can be certain that was true. Luke concludes, "And Jesus grew in wisdom and stature, and in favor with God and men" (2:52).

The Baptism of Jesus

Luke explains that it was during the period when John was traveling around the country of the Jordan, preaching a baptism of repentance for the forgiveness of sins, that people were coming in large crowds to be baptized (Luke 3:3). Matthew adds:

> Then Jesus came from Galilee to the Jordan to be baptized by John. But John tried to deter him, saying, 'I need to be baptized by you, and do you come to me?' Jesus replied, 'Let it be so now, it is proper for us to do this to fulfill all righteousness' (3:13-15).

With this, John consented, and Jesus was baptized. The moment he came up out of the water,

> He saw the Spirit of God descending like a dove and lighting on him. And a voice from heaven said, 'This is my Son, whom I love; with him I am well pleased' (vv:16,17).

The Temptation of Jesus

Following Jesus' baptism in the Jordan River, he "was led up by the Spirit into the desert to be tempted

> by the devil" (Matthew 4:1). Note that it was the Spirit of God, not the devil, who led him into the wilderness to be tempted. What was the reason for the Spirit's action? The question of authority and who was in control needed to be settled without delay. The time was right and the Lord's answer, "It is written," should have ended the conversation with the devil. Satan, however, is not inclined to be defeated or give up so easily. The encounter began immediately following Jesus' fast that lasted forty days and nights.

What better time to bring up the subject of food than when one is terribly hungry? Who other than Satan himself, just happened to be waiting for the opportune moment to put the Lord to the test? Satan used a subtle approach. Instead of asking, "'Why don't you just turn these stones into bread and eat?"—he presented a challenge. "If you are the Son of God, tell these stones to become bread" (v. 3). Jesus did not accept Satan's temptation but refused on the basis of Scriptural authority: "It is written, man does not live on bread alone, but on every word that comes from the mouth of God" (v. 4).

For the second temptation, Satan took Jesus into the holy city (Jerusalem) and had him stand on the pinnacle of the temple. He challenged Jesus to throw himself down, saying: "It is written," quoting from Psalm 91:11, 12. Jesus responded in the same way that he did with the first temptation: "It is also written: 'Do not put the Lord your God to the test'' (v. 7).

A third and final test came with the devil taking Jesus to a very high mountain. There, he displayed before him "all the kingdoms of the world and their splendor" (v. 8). "All this I will give you if you will bow down and worship me" (v. 9). One can almost hear the Lord raise his voice to a high pitch: "Away from me Satan! For it is written: 'Worship the Lord your God, and serve him only'" (v.10).

There are several thoughts to be gained from this encounter, all of which are important, but the one that stands out beyond and above all the rest is repeated three times: "It is written!" We can never go wrong following what is "written." However, this response assumes we are familiar with what is written and know who is speaking. Keep in mind that Satan can quote Scripture, as he did here. When the temptation ended, angels came and ministered to Jesus.

Summary

The Messianic concept appears early in the prophetic writings of the Old Testament. Moses assured the people that God would raise up a prophet whose word would be final.

Isaiah wrote of a virgin who would bear a son to be named Immanuel. Micah identified the town, Bethlehem, where he would be born.

The people were anticipating a Messiah, but his arrival had little in common with their expectation since his parents were common, ordinary people from the wrong location, Galilee.

The report was being circulated that Jesus was an illegitimate child. The story was refuted by his parents who had received a divine revelation from God regarding his miraculous conception by the Holy Spirit.

Events that transpired during his childhood clearly proved him to be an extraordinary child.

Jesus' temptation by Satan served to establish his authority as the Son of God while demonstrating his power over the devil. Each temptation was refuted with Scripture—"It is written."

Chapter three explains why Jesus left heaven and came down to the earth as a human being.

Jesus Christ left heaven and Came Down to the earth to save us from sin, something no human being could do. (John 3:17).

What was and is impossible for man to do, God did and continues to do through Jesus (John 6:38, 39).

CHAPTER 3

Why Did Jesus Christ Come Into the World?

Sincere religious people are frequently heard to ask: "Why was it necessary for Jesus to come to the earth? Couldn't God, who created this universe, have arranged another way to remove our sins without putting Jesus through the agony he suffered leading up to death on Calvary's cross?"

The reality is: *"There was no other way!"* The justice of God demanded a supreme sacrifice be made by one who was *perfect,* who *had never committed a sin,* as payment for removal of our transgressions. Jesus Christ, alone, was able to satisfy the justice of God and thereby free us from the punishment of sin.

While on the earth, Jesus taught a new way of living that included purity, honesty, humility, simplicity, integrity, sincerity and other things pertaining to godliness.

John quotes Jesus as saying, "For I have come down from heaven not to do my will but to do the will of him who sent me" (John 6:38). He expands on the thought that the Father's will is for all to look to Jesus, His Son, believe in him in order to have eternal life and be raised up at the last day (John 6:35-40).

Near the end of his gospel the apostle wrote,

> Jesus did many other miraculous signs in the presence of his disciples, which are not recorded in this book. But these are written that you may believe that Jesus is the Christ, the Son of God, and that by believing you may have life in his name (John 20:30-31).

On one occasion when Jesus was passing through Jericho, he came upon a man named Zacchaeus, a chief tax collector who was very wealthy. He was anxious to see this carpenter but was unable, because he was short in stature and a large crowd had gathered around Jesus. He solved the problem by running ahead of the crowd and climbing a sycamore tree. When Jesus approached the tree, he looked up and invited Zacchaeus to come down, declaring that he was going to dine at his house that day.

The people accused Jesus of being the guest of a sinner. Jesus' decision prompted Zacchaeus to make a remarkable confession, "Look, Lord! Here and now I give half of my possessions to the poor, and if I have cheated anybody out of anything, I will pay back four times the amount" (Luke 19:8).

What a confession! He obviously was sincere because Jesus responded, "Today salvation has come to this house.... For the Son of Man came to seek and to save what was lost" (vv. 9, 10). Please observe that Jesus came not only to save lost humanity but to seek the lost. That was his mission. The Lord's use of the word *lost,* was his way of indicating that the person was without God and without hope relating to one's eternal life. Unless there is a resolve in one's mind to change direction and follow Jesus, the Lord cannot reign over that person.

Jesus' approach to reaching and saving the lost was characterized by a genuine urgency. He emphasized putting kingdom business first (Matthew 6:33), as illustrated in the parable of the lost sheep, the lost coin, and the lost son (Luke chapter 15). Nothing took precedent over reaching the lost with the gospel, including saying farewell to family or burying the dead (Luke 9:57-62).

Related to salvation of the human race lost in sin without a Savior, is the problem of satisfying the *justice* of God. Since God is holy and righteous—a perfect being without sin—he cannot ignore or tolerate the presence of sin. Furthermore, we cannot offer anything sufficient to satisfy God's justice. The necessary requirement was the sacrifice of one who was perfect, who had never sinned—a requirement that eliminated the entire human race. Only one individual was qualified to be the sacrifice: Jesus Christ, the one and only unique Son of God. He willingly left heaven, came to the earth, lived a perfect life and sacrificed himself on Calvary's cross to atone for the sins of humanity. Remove this event from world history and no one could be saved.

Jesus' Ministry Begins

The encounter with Satan served to launch Jesus' public ministry. It is interesting that his message began with the same words used by John the Baptist, "Repent, for the kingdom of heaven is near" (Matthew 4:17).

Why Start With Repentance?

Since faith is considered the beginning point with Christianity, why did Jesus tell his audience to "repent"? In answering this question, it is essential to keep in mind that for generations the Israelite nation had been considered God's chosen people. As such, they were looked upon as people of faith, who believed in God and were without the need of teaching regarding faith. In reality, they had departed from the original teachings and needed to change direction, turn away from sin and turn back to God. Of course, they knew about God and had received multiple blessings for generations, but they also had disobeyed and turned away to engage in sinful behavior, continually. They needed a change of heart and mind, the very thing repentance is all about. Until repentance occurs, Jesus Christ cannot reign in the heart.

The Lord's commission was limited to the Israelite nation in the beginning. When Jesus chose the twelve disciples to preach the gospel, his instruction was, "Do not go among the Gentiles or enter any town of the Samaritans. Go rather to the lost sheep of Israel" (Matthew 10:5, 6).

The Great Commission, which included all nations and all people, was not proclaimed until the end of Jesus' public ministry, following his resurrection from the tomb. Mark's account of this "Commission" is stated as follows:

> Go into all the world and preach the good news to all creation. Whoever believes and is baptized will be saved, but whoever does not believe will be condemned (Mark 16:15, 16).

Matthew's account of the "Great Commission" is found in chapter 28:18-20. As noted, response to the message was to begin with faith. Luke gives the implementation of this Great Commission's command to go "into all the world" in Acts, chapter ten (Acts 13:46).

Jesus' Power to Draw Men to Himself

Jesus' selection of the men to follow and become his disciples is a remarkable event. Mark records Jesus walking beside the Sea of Galilee, where he came upon Simon Peter and his brother Andrew engaged in fishing, which was their daily business for making a living. Jesus simply calls out to them: "Come follow me and I will make you fishers of men" (Mark 1:17). The immediate response of these men to abandon their nets and begin to follow Jesus is an act that one would not expect. Jesus walks a little further and encounters James and his brother John, both sons of Zebedee, out in a boat. Without delay, he called them and they immediately left their father, Zebedee, and their hired servants in the boat and followed Jesus along with Peter and Andrew.

Luke records the call of Levi, the tax collector. Jesus found Levi sitting at the tax booth. "Follow me," were the only words spoken, "and Levi got up, left everything, and followed him" (Luke 5:27, 28). The remarkable manner in which Mark and Luke describe these calls to be a disciple is quite amazing. Did these men have previous knowledge about Jesus, his family or his unusual birth? Possibly, but the gospel accounts do not address this question. We probably would refuse someone approaching us and calling: "Follow me," without a clear explanation as to why.

In discussing this with my granddaughter, I asked her what her response would have been. First, you need to know that she is a devout Christian who truly loves the Lord. Without hesitation, she replied, "I would have said, you must be out of your mind." Her answer probably is not far from the response of most people.

What was there about Jesus that so electrified these men and caused them suddenly to leave family, friends, and their occupation to follow him? Certainly it was not his physical appearance, because Isaiah's prophecy described him as having "no beauty or majesty to attract us to him, nothing in his appearance that we should desire him" (Isaiah 53:2b). Nor did they follow him because of his family's prestige. His parents were plain, ordinary people from the city of Nazareth in Galilee.

If these men were familiar with the events described by Matthew (chapter four)—Jesus' preaching the good news of the kingdom throughout Galilee in the synagogue, healing every disease and sickness among the people—we can understand why they accepted the invitation. It is true that following the above comment, Matthew wrote:

> News about him spread all over Syria, and people brought to him all who were ill with various diseases,

> those suffering severe pain, the demon possessed, those having seizures, and the paralyzed, and he healed them. Large crowds from Galilee, the Decapolis, Jerusalem, Judea and the region across the Jordan followed him (Matthew 4:23-25).

The men, who accepted Jesus' call, may also have been familiar with Mark's comment that the people were amazed at his teaching because he taught them as one having authority and not as the teachers of the law. Mark also stated that news regarding Jesus spread rapidly throughout the entire region of Galilee (Mark 1:22, 28). From these remarks, it seems reasonable to conclude that these men may have had considerable information regarding the carpenter from Galilee. In addition, being divine, Jesus' ministry was reinforced with the continuous presence of the Holy Spirit. There is the additional comment by Luke that, "He was filled with wisdom and the grace of God was upon him" (Luke 2:40). Combine all of the above evidence and it becomes easier to understand why Peter, Andrew, James, John and Levi would readily accept Jesus' call to "Follow me."

The fact that Jesus immediately began to solicit help in spreading his message by selecting twelve disciples demonstrates his sense of urgency in spreading the message. Without delay, Jesus and his disciples traveled throughout Galilee visiting the Jewish synagogues with his message focused on the "gospel of the kingdom" (v.23). Luke records his emphatic declaration: "I must preach the kingdom of God to the other cities also, for *I was sent for this purpose*" (Luke 4:43, emphasis added). This message is consistent with Luke's account that the Son of Man came to seek and to save the lost.

Matthew records that Jesus gave the twelve disciples "authority to drive out evil spirits and to heal every disease and sickness" (Matthew 10:1). They were to "Heal the sick, raise the dead, cleanse those who have leprosy and drive out demons. Freely you have received, freely give" (v.8).

Test of Discipleship

On one occasion, when Jesus and the disciples were walking along the road, a man commented that he would follow Jesus wherever he went. The Master turned and said, "Follow Me." The man's reply was, "Permit me first to go and bury my father" (Luke 9:59). This request appears to be reasonable, as it was to the men whom Jesus called to follow him. However, the Lord's response was: "Allow the dead to bury their own dead; but as for you, go and proclaim everywhere the kingdom of God" (v.60, NASV).

The same words were issued to a second man who declared: "I will follow You, Lord, but first permit me to say good-bye to those at home" (v. 61, NASV). Again, Jesus' reply is shocking. "No one, after putting his hand to the plow and looking back, is fit for the kingdom of God" (v. 62, NASV). The people of that generation were not accustomed to such bold assertions—and neither are we today. It is amusing to observe how we gloss over such remarks. Most Bible scholars have limited comments on these passages, other than stating that the Master is emphasizing the urgency of kingdom business.

News about the ministry of Jesus spread rapidly throughout the territories of Syria, Galilee, the Decapolis, Jerusalem, Judea and beyond the Jordan River. In addition to the message of this itinerant preacher, he healed people of various diseases and sicknesses (Matthew 4:23-25).

Authority Recognized by the Multitude

The authenticity of Jesus' teaching, compared to others, was clear to the multitude that sat on the mountain side and listened to what is referred to as the Sermon on the Mount, recorded by Matthew in chapters five through seven. At the conclusion, the people were amazed because he taught them "as one having authority, and not as their scribes" (Matthew 7:28, 29).

More evidence was soon to follow with his "I AM" comments:

- "I am the bread of life. He who comes to me will never go hungry, and he who believes in me will never be thirsty" (John 6:35).
- "I am the light of the world. Whoever follows me will never walk in darkness, but will have the light of life" (8:12).
- "I am the good shepherd; I know my sheep and my sheep know me" (10:14).
- "I am the resurrection and the life. He who believes in me will live, even though he dies; and whoever lives and believes in me will never die" (11:25).
- "I am the way and the truth and the life. No one comes to the Father except through me" (14:6).

These daily bold assertions furnished additional evidence to justify his claims that he truly was the Son of God.

Summary

The reason Jesus Christ left heaven and came to the earth was to save and deliver the human race from sin.

God's justice demanded that a perfect sacrifice be made to atone or pay for our sins, but none existed on earth; consequently, the sinless Son of God graciously agreed to take our place and be punished for our sins.

To demonstrate his humanity, Jesus was born to the virgin, Mary. To assure his divinity, he was conceived by the Holy Spirit and not by Joseph.

> Most of what he did and taught—including a variety of miracles—portrayed supernatural power and authority. These factors obviously influenced the decision of the twelve disciples to drop everything and immediately turn to follow Jesus.
>
> Jesus' method of testing the sincerity of a disciple appeared strange to many then and now. Not taking time to say "good-by" to family members or "putting the hand to the plow without looking back" sounds extreme to most of us.
>
> The Lord spoke numerous parables to express urgency in reaching the lost.

The next chapter looks at how Jesus taught, causing educators to label him "The Master Teacher."

Jesus Christ is called "The Master Teacher" Why?

He was given "All Authority" by God.

"Then Jesus came to them and said, "'All authority in heaven and on earth has been given to me" (Matthew 28:18).

Things that are impossible with man are possible with God (Mark 10:27).

Chapter 4

Jesus, the Master Teacher

1. Jesus was A Master Teacher

Not only did Jesus teach as one having authority, but his use of parables, analogies and illustrations made it easy for common citizens to grasp religious concepts. For example, Jesus talked about the farmer sowing seed, which he compared to the word of God. He then compared the soil on which the seed fell to our hearts as receptors for the word that was sown. He proceeded to contrast the good soil to the receptive mind that received the word and yielded fruit (Matthew 13:1-23).

By using illustrations that most of his listeners understood, the people could grasp the concept of God's Word as a seed that produced a spiritual fruit in their lives. Consequently, they could compare their reception of God's Word to one of four soils in which seed would grow. Teaching by Pharisees and other religious leaders, on the other hand, largely consisted of scholarship treatises that showed off their research skills and learning. Analysis of rabbis' writings arguing over details of the Law of Moses was the major content of the teaching. No wonder that Jesus' teaching was more popular and understandable by a society largely composed of illiterate citizens who could not read and comprehend the written analysis and debates of learned scholars.

In Luke chapter fifteen, Jesus introduced the parables of the Lost Sheep, the Lost Coin and the Lost Son, which emphasized how precious one soul is to the Lord. In the Lost Sheep parable, the shepherd with a hundred sheep, who was missing one lamb, left the ninety-nine safely in the fold and searched for the one lost lamb until he found it. Jesus reemphasized the same principle in the Lost Coin parable: the woman with ten silver coins loses one, so she lit a lamp, swept and searched the house until she recovered the missing coin. In the most famous of the three parables—the prodigal (or lost) son—Jesus drives home the same principle. The story of the Lost Son and the loving Father covers a number of vital lessons. This approach to teaching was very effective to his listeners.

2. Jesus Was A Gentle Teacher

Jesus was a gentle, loving teacher, as seen in his treatment of the Samaritan woman, whom he met at the well dug by Jacob in Sychar, when she came to draw water. Jesus engaged her in conversation knowing that she was a sinful woman, who had lived with a series of five husbands; in fact, her present "partner" was not her husband, either. Many preachers in today's society would have felt justified in immediately condemning this woman for her immoral behavior. Jesus, however, began a conversation about living water that will lead to eternal life (John 4:12, 14). In effect, Jesus offered her a new life from the blessings that were available from a different type of water and knowledge of the Messiah. In short, he convicted her to the degree that she rushed into the city of Samaria to tell others of her experience. As a result, many townspeople followed her back to the well to meet and listen to Jesus. John writes: "Many of the Samaritans believed in him because of the woman's testimony" (John 4:39).

3. Jesus Was Kind Even To Strangers

On one occasion when Jesus and his disciples were approaching the city of Jericho, a blind man was sitting by the roadside begging.

When the crowd came near where the beggar was sitting, he asked what was happening. When he was told that Jesus of Nazareth was passing by, the beggar called out, "Jesus, Son of David, have mercy on me!" (Luke 18:38). From this remark, it is obvious that the man had some knowledge of Scripture because he referred to David. He also knew that Jesus was associated with the lineage of David because he referred to him as the "Son" of David.

The person leading the way told the beggar to be quiet, but this prompted him to shout loudly, "Son of David, have mercy on me!" (v.39b). Notice that in both comments the blind man used the word "mercy." Not only did he need help; he was also humble in the way he made his appeal to Jesus. When he was nearby, Jesus asked, "What do you want me to do for you?" (v. 41b). This question was not asked because the Lord did not know what the man needed. It was important that all in the crowd hear his response.

Question: Why did Jesus say to the beggar: "Your *faith* has healed you?" Answer: It was not a requirement for the man to have faith for Jesus to be able to restore his vision, but it was important for the Lord to acknowledge him as a man of faith who left the scene praising God.

Luke explains that the blind man immediately received his sight, and following Jesus, was showing his gratitude by praising God, along with all the people who had witnessed the miracle (Luke 18:43).

This story calls to memory the admonition of Paul to the Ephesians:

> "Be kind and compassionate to one another, forgiving each other, just as in Christ God forgave you" (Ephesians 4:32).

4. Jesus Extended Compassion To The Poor And Downtrodden

Mark records the occasion of a man with leprosy who approached Jesus, fell to his knees and begged the Lord to heal him. In Israeli society, because of the Law of Moses, a person with leprosy was required to call out "unclean" when approaching another individual. This man began by saying: "If you are willing, you can make me clean" (Mark 1:40). This poor man's condition reminds us of the African Ebola virus epidemic. People with the virus are going to be avoided by others for fear of catching the disease.

The Lord's response was quite remarkable. Mark states that, "Filled with compassion, Jesus reached out his hand and touched the man." '"I am willing,'" he said, "Be clean!" (Mark 1:41). One might say, "But Jesus had no fear of contracting leprosy." That is true, but would he have touched the man if this were not the case? My answer is, "Absolutely!" Without delay, the leper was healed. The Lord warned him not to tell others, knowing what the psychological affect would be. However, the healed man could not wait to get out and share the wonderful news that his leprosy was gone.

5. Jesus Was Firm, Direct, Deliberate And Bold When Needed

The temple in Jerusalem was sacred to the Lord. Matthew records that Jesus entered the temple to find moneychangers desecrating the area. Out of anger, he drove out the merchants who were buying and selling. He overturned the tables of the moneychangers and those who were selling the doves. With this action, his words rang out: "It is written, my house will be called a house of prayer; but you are making it a den of robbers" (Matthew 21:12, 13). No one made an effort to contradict Jesus' statement because they knew it to be true.

The Parable of the Pharisee and the Tax Collector illustrates Jesus' firm, direct and deliberate method of teaching. Jesus told of two men—a Pharisee and a tax collector—who visited the temple to pray. The Pharisee's prayer was shocking: "God I thank you that I am not like other men—robbers, evil doers, adulterers—or even like this tax collector" (Luke 18:11). He continued his prayer by reminding

God about his fasting and alms giving, as though God might have forgotten. His entire prayer centered on what a wonderful person he was. Furthermore, he was thanking God for the wrong reason—not for God's mercy, grace, goodness and loving kindness—but for his being an outstanding individual.

The tax collector, on the other hand, kept his distance from the Pharisee, but was close enough to hear his prayer. He felt unworthy to look up toward heaven. Instead, he beat his breast—a sign of humility—while uttering this short, humble prayer: "God, have mercy on me, a sinner" (Luke 18:13). Four words spoken in this short sentence go to the heart of the man's need: God...me...mercy...sinner. He addressed the right source—*God*. He directed it to the appropriate need—*me, a sinner,* and begged for *mercy.* Jesus said that the tax collector returned home justified before God, ending his teaching with these words: "For everyone who exalts himself will be humbled, and he who humbles himself will be exalted" (v.14b).

6. Jesus Manifested A Servant Attitude Toward All

John records a touching scene in which Jesus was a model of a person who serves others (John 13:1-17). Late in his ministry, the Passover feast was approaching, and it was time for the evening meal. With all his disciples seated for the meal, Jesus got up, removed his outer clothing and wrapped a towel around his waist. He proceeded to pour water into a basin and washed the disciples' feet.

To keep this event in perspective, remember that Jesus was the Master and his disciples were his servants. In Jesus' time, a servant was trained and obligated to wash his master's feet. When an invited guest arrived, it was considered an act of courtesy to wash his feet. No plan had been arranged by the disciples to perform this task; besides, the disciples had been arguing over "which of them was considered to be the greatest" (Luke 22:24). Thus, they were in no mood to wash each other's feet. Jesus gave them a model of being a true servant that his disciples would not forget. Jesus even washed the feet of Judas, who would betray him that night.

Peter evidently realized that the disciples had failed and were negligent in their master-servant relationship. Thus, Peter responded with a negative, emphatic objection when Jesus approached to wash his feet: "You shall never wash my feet" (John 13:8). The exchange that followed is truly revealing concerning the Master's attitude of service. The reader is encouraged to turn to John 13:1-17 and absorb these inspirational thoughts by reading all of this passage.

7. Jesus Loved Little Children

A song frequently sung in our assemblies superbly sets the tone for this section of our study:

> Jesus loves the little children,
> All the children of the world,
> Red and yellow, black and white,
> They are precious in His sight—
> Jesus loves the little children of the world.

Luke described an event when people brought babies to Jesus so that he could touch them. Parents had observed the results that occurred when Jesus laid his hands on the sick; perhaps they were expecting something special to happen. Their actions provoked the disciples to the point that they rebuked the adults who were bringing the children. The Lord's response probably shocked the disciples because he invited the children to come: "Let the children come to me, and do not hinder them, for the kingdom of God belongs to such as these" (Luke 18:16). He further declared that to enter the kingdom, one must possess the attitude of a child.

On another occasion, a child was a wonderful object lesson for the disciples. Mark records the disciples' arguing among themselves as to which one of them was the greatest disciple. Jesus settled the discussion by calling a child and standing him among them. Taking the child in his arms he declared:

> Whoever welcomes one of these little children in my name welcomes me; and whoever welcomes me does not welcome me but the one who sent me (Mark 9:37).

What a marvelous way of teaching while *taking the wind out of their sails* without raising his voice.

8. Jesus Loved His Enemies

In teaching about relationships, Jesus gave instruction regarding enemies that may have been difficult for many of his disciples to obey:

> "Love your enemies, do good to those who hate you, bless those who curse you, pray for those who mistreat you" (Luke 6:27).

Jesus' command constitutes major challenges for Christians to accept and carry out. We are ordered to:

- love our enemies.
- do good to those who hate us.
- extend blessings to those who curse us.
- pray for those who mistreat us.

These commands may be more than some can stomach, but they are—pure and simple—words of Jesus. The thought ends with the words of the Golden Rule: "Do to others as you would have them do to you" (Luke 6:31). There is more before the chapter ends, but most of us will need time to dust ourselves off before jumping into the deeper concepts.

Summary

For generations people interested in becoming effective communicators have carefully examined the approach used by Jesus in his teaching. People, by the thousands, gathered around anxious to hang on to every word spoken by him.

Jesus made use of common illustrations, analogies and parables chosen from things the people observed daily. He took ideas from farming, tilling the soil, sowing the seed, watching the plants grow to maturity and through the use of parables would teach effective spiritual lessons. By comparing the sower, the seed and the soil to the word of God and a receptive mind, the lesson was caught quickly.

As a Master Teacher, he was careful not to be offensive when dealing with sensitive subjects. He knew how to apply the gentle touch when talking about topics like marriage and divorce.

Kindness and compassion were virtues used to soften the hearts of tax collectors and critical Pharisees. When the occasion called for boldness, being direct and firm, he could choose the words and demeanor to obtain the appropriate results. Driving out the moneychangers and those desecrating the temple perfectly illustrates this point.

Chapter five examines a few of the miracles Jesus performed that demonstrate he had come from God and possessed supernatural power. To turn water to wine; raise a dead person; walk on water; restore the vision of one who was blind; are not events that human beings can achieve apart from the supernatural. Not only did Jesus perform miracles, but he possessed the authority and power to pass on this ability to the apostles.

Jesus Christ Performed Miracles HE

1. **Turned water to wine**
2. **Walked on water**
3. **Fed 5000 with five loaves and two fish**
4. **Restored sight to the man born blind**
5. **Raised the Dead**

"What is impossible with men is possible with God" (Luke 18:27).

Chapter 5

Miracles Performed by Jesus

Throughout his public ministry, Jesus performed many miracles in conjunction with his teaching that validated his supernatural power and confirmed his claim to be "the Son of God."

It is appropriate to point out that the word "miracle" takes on an entirely different meaning in the vocabulary of many people today contrasted to its meaning in New Testament times.

The Random House Dictionary of the English Language, The Unabridged Edition: defines "miracle" as 1. an effect or extraordinary event in the physical world which surpasses all natural cause. 2. such an effect or event manifesting or considered as a work of God.[1] The miracles Jesus performed are not repeated or duplicated by so-called miracle workers today.

Turning Water to Wine

The first miracle occurred in Cana of Galilee at a wedding ceremony. Jesus was a guest along with his mother and his disciples. A large crowd must have been in attendance because the host ran out of wine. Interesting enough, the mother of Jesus informed Jesus that, "They have no more wine" (John 2:3). It was obvious that Mary expected Jesus to remedy the situation. He first answered by asking why she would involve him in the matter, since his time had not yet arrived. Despite his apparent lack of interest in solving the problem, she told the servants to, "Do whatever he tells you" (v.5).

Six large, stone water jars stood nearby that were used by the Jews for ceremonial washing, each having a capacity of twenty to thirty gallons. Jesus instructed the servants to fill the jars completely with water. Afterward, they were to draw some out and take it to the master of the banquet. When he tasted the water now turned to wine, he called the bridegroom over and wanted to know why this choice wine was not served first to the guests.

Walking on Water

On another occasion, Jesus had just completed the feeding of about five thousand hungry men gathered in a very remote place. Immediately afterward, he directed the disciples to get into a boat and travel to the opposite side of the lake while he dismissed the crowd. As the disciples attempted to cross the lake, a storm arose and the boat was buffeted by strong winds. In the midst of the storm, Jesus came walking on the water. When the disciples saw him they were terrified because they believed that his image was a ghost. Without delay, he relieved their fears by saying, "Take courage! It is I. Don't be afraid" (Matthew 14:27).

Peter, who was always the first to speak, said, "Lord, if it's you," "tell me to come to you on the water" (Matthew 14:28). It is clear from the way the apostle spoke that he was not totally certain that the image was Jesus. Fortunately for Peter and those in the boat with him, Jesus answered with one word, "Come." Peter obeyed, jumped out of the boat and began walking toward the Master. For a moment all went well until he felt the wind striking against his body. Suddenly, he became afraid, took his eyes off of Jesus, and he began to sink. He cried out for the Lord to save him, which Jesus did by extending his hand and raising him up.

Jesus used this occasion to teach a very useful lesson. He chided Peter's lack of faith and asked, "why did you doubt?" (Matthew 14:31). Doubt arises when fear enters our minds and we take our eyes off of Jesus. Once Jesus and Peter were in the boat, the winds died down and all was calm. This event ended as the men in the boat worshiped Jesus and stated emphatically, "Truly you are the Son of God" (v.33).

Healing Many of Illness and Disease

Once, when Jesus and his disciples had crossed the lake, they landed the boat at Gennesaret. As soon as the local men recognized Jesus, they spread the word around the area. Matthew adds: "People brought all their sick to him and begged him to let the sick just touch the edge of his cloak, and all who touched him were healed" (Matthew 14:35-36). This account is one of many reported in the Gospels in which Jesus was asked to heal people of various afflictions. It is one more example of his divine power to perform miracles.

Jesus Calms the Storm

Mark, in his gospel, covers an event that became very personal for the disciples. They were in the boat and Jesus had been presenting numerous lessons through parables. Jesus proposed leaving the crowd and going over to the other side of the lake. On the way he went to the back of the boat and fell asleep. A heavy storm came up that caused the waves to break over the boat. The disciples became very uneasy and quickly woke Jesus. Their question to the Master certainly demonstrated their anxiety. "Teacher, don't you care if we drown?" (Mark 4:38). For men who had witnessed numerous miracles, this question appears rather awkward. But then, is it? Fortunately for these men, Jesus was present. He got up, rebuked the wind and with three words, '"Quiet! Be still!'"(v.39), all became completely calm. The

Lord's *first question* is not too shocking. '"Why are you so afraid?'" You see, they were faced with sudden death in their minds, so fear was a natural instinct. The *second question* really cut to the heart. '"Do you still have no faith?'" Notice: Jesus did not say, "What has happened to your faith?" He is talking to men who *still* have *no faith*. That comment had to hurt.

Here is a situation where they have been with Jesus daily for quite some time and have observed him do the impossible as they viewed it. They had seen him turn water to wine; feed 5000 from five loaves and two fish; walk on water; etc. Why the doubt that this time would be any different? Take note that here Mark records, "They were terrified and asked each other, '"Who is this? Even the winds and the waves obey him!'"

Before getting too critical, perhaps this question deserves an answer: "If I had been one of the people present on that occasion, would my response have been any different?"

Restoring Sight to the Blind

The four gospel narratives record many examples of Jesus restoring sight to the blind, one involving a man born blind. One day while Jesus was walking along with his disciples, he encountered a man who had been blind from birth. Upon seeing him, the disciples asked a serious question: "Rabbi, who sinned, this man or his parents, that he was born blind?" (John 9: 2). They obviously associated the man's blindness with one of two causes: his personal sin or his parents' sin, which meant that the man's handicap was the result of some evil act performed by his parents before his birth. Since the man was born blind, guilt from his sin could not have caused his blindness. He had done nothing to create guilt. Jesus' answer must have surprised them, since he stated that neither the man nor his parents had sinned. Instead, "this happened so that the work of God might be displayed in his life" (v.3).

The manner in which Jesus handled this event was unusual. He spat on the ground, made some mud with the saliva and put it on the man's eyes. He then instructed him to go wash in the pool of Siloam, which the man did. As expected, he came away able to see.

This miracle created quite a stir once the word got around that the blind man, who used to sit and beg, was now able to see. Neighbors and others in the community, who regularly saw the man begging, were asking, "Isn't this the same man who used to sit and beg?" Some agreed while others stated that he only looked like him (vv. 8, 9). The person that was healed insisted that he was the man.

The healed man was taken to the Pharisees, who were determined to find out the truth of three questions:

- Was he the man who was born blind?
- How was he now able to see?
- Did Jesus violate the Law of Moses by performing work on the Sabbath day?

The Pharisees concluded that Jesus had violated the law by performing work on the Sabbath. When asked how he received his sight? The man replied: "He put mud on my eyes...and I washed, and now I see" (v. 15).

The controversy raged between the Pharisees, who accused Jesus of being a sinner, and the man's parents who insisted that the former blind man was their son. For fear of being cast out of the Synagogue, the parents placed the burden of answering the Pharisees' questions on their son by stating that, "He is of age; he will speak for himself" (v.21).

The Pharisees summoned the man a second time, saying, "We know this man is a sinner." "Give glory to God" (v.24). His reply only added to the Pharisees anger because it rejected their final judgment of the event. "Whether he is a sinner or not, I don't know. One thing I do know. I was blind but now I see!" (v. 25). This story—found in John

9:1-41—is an inspiration to read because it reveals Jesus' true nature along with his supernatural power.

The event also raises an interesting question: Was it necessary for Jesus to make mud and rub it on the blind man's eyes before he could see? The answer is, obviously "no"; however, Jesus' method of healing the blind man was the Lord's way of testing his faith. The lesson to be learned from this example is: When the Lord speaks, we must listen and obey, if we expect results.

Raising Dead Lazarus

The resurrection of Lazarus—recorded in John 11:1-54—is one of three occasions in which Jesus restored life to a dead person. Lazarus lived in the village of Bethany with his two sisters, Mary and Martha, and he became very ill. The sisters sent word to Jesus that their brother was sick. The Lord discussed this matter with his disciples, declaring that this sickness would not end in death but was for God's glory (vv.1-16).

Jesus' decision to travel to Judea was not received enthusiastically by his disciples because the Jews had earlier attempted to stone him. He explained to them that their friend Lazarus had fallen asleep and he needed to go awaken him. Further comment prompted Jesus to state emphatically: "Lazarus is dead, and for your sake I am glad I was not there, so that you may believe. But let us go to him."

Upon arriving in Judea, Jesus was told that Lazarus had been buried in the tomb for four days. Martha, the first to meet Jesus, manifested her strong belief in the Lord's power: "Lord",.. "if you had been here, my brother would not have died. But I know that even now God will give you whatever you ask" (vv. 21, 22). Jesus' response was partially what she expected, but not altogether. He said: "Your brother will rise again." Martha believed Jesus' declaration, but she was thinking of the resurrection that would take place at the last day. The Lord's answer probably was more than she anticipated, for he declared: "I am the resurrection and the life. He who believes in me will live, even though he dies; and whoever lives and believes in me will never die. Do you believe this?" (v.26).

Jesus' question was a challenge for Martha to answer. How was she to respond, for she knew that her brother was dead? Rather than answer directly, she affirmed her faith in Jesus, "I believe that you are the Christ, the Son of God, who was to come into the world." Her answer did not contradict what Jesus had said, which included more information than she was able to comprehend at that moment.

She quickly went to tell her sister, "The Teacher is here...and is asking for you." Mary went to Jesus where he waited outside the village. Once there, she fell at his feet and repeated Martha's earlier statement, "Lord, if you had been here, my brother would not have died." When Jesus saw Mary and those who accompanied her weeping, he was moved deeply and troubled in spirit. John reports that, "Jesus wept" (v.35). This verse is the shortest sentence in Scripture.

Jesus' weeping prompted numerous observations by those who had gathered at the tomb. Some commented on how Jesus loved Lazarus. Others were critical of Jesus, questioning why this man, who had opened the eyes of the blind, failed to heal Lazarus and prevent his death.

Jesus then asked to be taken to Lazarus' tomb where a large stone covered its opening. Jesus ordered that the stone be removed, which prompted Martha to speak up and say, "...by this time there is a bad odor, for he has been there four days," confirming to all present that Lazarus truly was dead. Jesus was prompted to say, "Did I not tell you that if you believed, you would see the glory of God?"

With the stone removed,

> Jesus looked up and said, Father, I thank you that you have heard me. I knew that you always hear me, but I said this for the benefit of the people standing here, that they may believe that you sent me (vv. 41, 42).

Note that every word uttered by Jesus was for the benefit of the people, not for his sake. The stage was set; Jesus called out in a loud voice, "Lazarus, come out!" (v. 43). Question: Was there a brief delay before the dead man exited alive? Perhaps. At any rate, the people were witnessing an undeniable miracle: a live person appeared at the entrance of the tomb—a man who had been buried in the tomb for four days. His hands and feet were wrapped with strips of linen and his face was covered with a cloth. This provides further evidence that the man had been dead. There was no movement by the crowd until Jesus said, "Take off the grave clothes and let him go" (v. 44).

This miracle created a mixed response by the crowd. Some believed and put their trust in Jesus. Others hastily went to the Pharisees and reported Jesus' miracle and how Lazarus had come out of the tomb. This report prompted the Chief Priests and Pharisees to hastily call a meeting of the Sanhedrin. Once assembled, no effort was made to deny or reject the report as delivered to them. They admitted that Jesus had performed miraculous signs; thus, any attempt to deny the validity of this event would have them labeled as hypocrites. So they agreed, "If we let him go on like this, everyone will believe in him, and then the Romans will come and take away both our place and our nation" (v. 48).

So, the chief priests made plans to kill both Jesus and Lazarus, since many of the Jews were turning to trust in Jesus as a result of Lazarus' resurrection. Consequently, Jesus restricted his movement among the Jews and withdrew to a region near the desert to a village named Ephraim, where he stayed with his disciples (vv. 51-54).

Summary

> The miracles performed by Jesus have little in common with what faith healers are observed doing today or in any age. The Lord dealt with miracles and events that could be verified.

Turning water to wine in large quantities cannot be faked. Neither can walking on a huge body of water be achieved without supernatural help.

The apostle Peter learned that lesson (Matthew 14:30). It was Peter who explained to Cornelius and his family that "God anointed Jesus of Nazareth with the Holy Spirit and power" (Acts 10:38), providing him with the ability to perform miracles.

The authenticity of the miracles Jesus performed was easy to check. Restoring a withered hand, giving sight to a blind person, raising a dead man who had been in the tomb four days, demanded a miracle. The chief priest and Pharisees knew all too well the truth of this matter. (John 11:47, 48).

Peter reminded Cornelius and his household "how God anointed Jesus of Nazareth with the *Holy Spirit and power,* and how he went around doing good and healing all who were under the power of the devil, because God was with him" (Acts 10:38, emphasis added).

Chapter six covers events that include the death and resurrection of Jesus.

God Raised Jesus from the Tomb

"The angel said to the women, 'Do not be afraid, for I know that you are looking for Jesus, who was crucified. He is not here; he has risen, just as he said. Come and see the place where he lay. Then go quickly and tell his disciples: He has risen from the dead and is going ahead of you into Galilee'" (Matthew 28:5, 6).

"Jesus looked at them and said, 'With man this is impossible, but with God all things are possible'"(Matthew 19:26).

Chapter 6

Events Covering Death and Resurrection of Jesus

As reported at the closing of the last chapter, the religious leaders planned to kill Jesus after the resurrection of Lazarus. Killing Lazarus also was considered, which would be the second time for him to die.

Betrayal by Judas

During the Passover Feast Jesus informed his disciples that the time was near for him to depart this world and return to the Father. While they were sharing the evening meal, Jesus appeared troubled in spirit and testified, '"I tell you the truth, one of you is going to betray me"' (John 13:21). As expected, the disciples began to look at each other wondering which one he meant. Since "the disciple whom Jesus loved" (referring to John), was reclining next to Jesus, Peter motioned for him to ask Jesus which one he meant. "Jesus answered," '"It is the one to whom I give this piece of bread when I have dipped it in the dish"' (vv.25, 26). The bread was given to Judas Iscariot, after which it is stated "Satan entered into him" (v.27). Then Jesus told him, '"What you are about to do, do quickly"' (v.27b).

Declaration of the Coming Holy Spirit

Jesus knew that, once he explained to the twelve his intention to return to the Father, they would be devastated and sorely grieved. Consequently, he had begun planting thoughts of his death early in his ministry to prepare them for that day. John records Jesus' declaration that they would not at that time be able to come to where he was going (John 13:33-36). He followed up with comforting thoughts and great assurance that he was going to prepare a place for his people. He assured them that he would return and take them to his dwelling place (John 14:1-3).

Following this admonition, Jesus introduced his instruction regarding the Holy Spirit:

> All this I have spoken while still with you. But the Counselor, the Holy Spirit whom the Father will send in my name, will teach you all things and remind you of everything I have said to you (vv. 25, 26).

These verses are packed with highly significant information. The Lord made two important points in preparing his disciples for the occasion when he would leave them and return to the Father.

1. In his absence, the Father would send the Holy Spirit, also known as the Counselor, (Greek, παράκλητος; translated in other versions as Comforter, Advocate).
2. The Holy Spirit would be sent in Jesus' name to teach them all things and to remind them of everything the Master had taught them. They would *not* be relying on their own memory for what they recalled and were taught, but could be certain of its accuracy and truthfulness.

The fact that really captures one's attention is Jesus repeating the above statement three times in one presentation. Obviously, the Lord did not need to repeat a thought to assure its accuracy and importance; however, to repeat the same point three times (chapters 14,15, & 16) in one sitting is most unusual.

> **First,** similar words are found in chapter 15:26, 27.
>
> **Second,** in chapter 16:1-15, Jesus expands the thought, Unless I go away, the Counselor will not come to you; but if I go, I will send him to you. When he comes, he will *convict the world of guilt in regard to sin* and *righteousness* and *judgment*: in regard to sin, because men do not believe in me; in regard to righteousness, because I am going to the Father, where you can see me no longer; and in regard to judgment, because the prince of this world now stands condemned (vv. 7-11, emphasis added).
>
> **Third,** the Holy Spirit is called "the Spirit of truth" who, when he comes, "he will guide you into all truth." In the Greek text, a definite article appears before the word "truth." There is more in vv. 12-16 that should be examined carefully.

Before moving away from what Jesus said in the above three chapters, it is vital to understand that Jesus was addressing the apostles. They are being told exactly what to expect and what would happen once he returned to the Father. The Holy Spirit would be sent to comfort them; to teach and guide them as they went forward to spread the truth of God's Word. *This teaching regarding the Holy Spirit was not then, nor is it now, intended for all Christians.* From the book of Acts to the end of Revelation, the writers frequently included information explaining the *presence,* the *purpose* and the *work* of the Holy Spirit in the life of the Christian. The reader is encouraged to study the work of the Holy Spirit in its context in order to understand the Spirit's presence, purpose and work.

Once the apostles were anointed with the Holy Spirit on the day of Pentecost, they would be Jesus' witnesses beginning in Jerusalem, moving on to Judea, then to Samaria and finally to the ends of the earth (Acts 1:8). Their mission was to carry the message of salvation to people all over the world. This endeavor would prove to be a monumental undertaking—a task they were by no means ready to assume without the Holy Spirit's help.

Luke explains that regarding times and dates, the Lord had stated clearly that these matters were left to the Father's discretion. They would know when the correct time arrived because the Holy Spirit would come upon them and equip them with special power (Acts 1:8).

Events Surrounding Jesus' Resurrection

The apostle John recorded Jesus' conversation with his disciples about his death and resurrection. He explained to them that he would be absent for a short period of time, after which they would see him again:

Now is your time of grief, but I will see you again and you will rejoice, and no one will take away your joy.... I came from the Father and entered the world; now I am leaving the world and going back to the Father (John 16:22 and 28).

All four gospel accounts extensively cover the death and resurrection of Jesus. In Mark's account, the Sabbath has ended and the women, including Mary Magdalene, Mary the mother of James and Salome purchased spices to anoint Jesus' body. Early on the first day of the week, as the sun was rising, they made their way to the tomb, asking themselves the question: How would they gain entrance to the tomb since the stone covering it was very large? Matthew's record provided the answer: a violent earth-quake occurred, during which an angel of the Lord came down from heaven, rolled the stone away and sat down on it. His appearance frightened the guards, who were shaking with fear.

The angel calmed the fear of the women by stating:

> I know that you are looking for Jesus, who was crucified. He is not here; he has risen, just as he said. Come and see the place where he lay (Matthew 28:5, 6).

The women were instructed by the angel to go immediately and tell Jesus' disciples that he would meet them in Galilee. While they were hurrying away to share the exciting news with his disciples, Jesus appeared to the women and said: "Greetings"... "They came to him, clasped his feet and worshiped him" (Matthew 28:9).

Once the word of Jesus' resurrection reached the apostles and the others, Luke wrote: "But they did not believe the women, because their words seemed to them like nonsense" (Luke 24:11). Obviously, the apostles failed to grasp Jesus' earlier statement: '"The Son of Man must be delivered into the hands of sinful men, be crucified and on the third day be raised again'" (Luke 24:7).

The disciples knew the power of God because they were present when Jesus called out in a commanding voice to Lazarus, who had been in the tomb for four days, "Lazarus, come out!" (John 11:43). The dead man immediately stood up before the crowd. Why then were they reluctant to accept the women's word? They chose, instead, to check it out for themselves. Peter and the disciple "whom Jesus loved" (referring to John, the apostle) ran to the tomb; John arrived first, but he waited for Peter to catch up before entering the tomb.

According to John's account, Simon Peter entered the tomb first. The burial clothes were in the tomb and folded neatly. The cloth that had been around Jesus' head was folded separately. John "saw and believed," but the two disciples "still did not understand from Scripture that Jesus had to rise from the dead" (John 20:8, 9). More evidence was needed and more would be provided.

Luke records an incident of Jesus' appearance after his resurrection to two men on their way to the village of Emmaus about seven miles from Jerusalem. They were discussing the day's happenings when suddenly Jesus appeared, walking along with them. Luke explains that they were kept from recognizing him. Jesus entered the conversation by asking what they were discussing as they were walking along. One of the men, Cleopas, was surprised that this visitor did not know the things that had recently taken place. An exchange of conversation then occurred:

Jesus: "What things?"

The two disciples: "About Jesus of Nazareth," the "... prophet, powerful in word and deed before God and all the people" (Luke 24:13-19).

The two disciples: They explained how the rulers had handed him over to be sentenced and to be crucified. They had hoped he was the one who would redeem Israel. Now some of the women had visited the tomb and did not find Jesus' body and saw a vision of angels, who reported that Jesus was alive.

Jesus chided them for failing to understand and believe the prophets, who had prophesied that the Christ would have to suffer these things before entering his glory. Beginning with Moses and the prophets, he explained what the Scripture revealed concerning himself.

As they approached the village of Emmaus, Jesus acted as though he intended to go on, but the two men urged him to stay with them, since night was approaching. He stayed and joined them for a meal.

Much to their surprise, when Jesus took bread, gave thanks, broke it and began to pass it around, their eyes were opened and they recognized him. Before a word was spoken, he disappeared from their sight.

The two disciples arose and returned to Jerusalem where they found the eleven disciples gathered with several others affirming the truth of the women's report that, indeed, the Lord had risen and had appeared to Simon (Luke 24:25-34). "Then the two told what had happened, and how Jesus was recognized by them when he broke the bread" (v.35).

Jesus Appears to the Disciples

While the disciples are still listening to Cleopas and his companion's story of meeting Jesus on the road to Emmaus, Jesus appeared among them with the words: "Peace be with you" (Luke 24:36). No wonder they were startled and frightened and thought they were seeing a *spirit.*

The Greek word used by Luke in the previous passage is *pneuma,* and is translated in the New International Version as "ghost". Why the translators chose to use the word *ghost* is an enigma since older English versions and more recent ones render "pneuma" as "spirit," including KJV, ASV, NASV, and Confraternity versions). It is true that the KJV uses both ghost and spirit in Acts 2:4 "And they were all filled with the Holy Ghost, (pneuma) and began to speak with other tongues, as the Spirit (pneuma) gave them utterance." This same Greek word is used in John 4:24: "God is spirit (*pneuma*) and his worshipers must worship in spirit (*pneuma*) and in truth."

The Greek word for ghost is *phantasma,* as recorded in Matthew 14:26 and Mark 6:49 and reads: "It is a ghost (*phantasma*)" when the disciples saw Jesus walking on the sea. It is little wonder that they cried out for fear and thought it was a ghost.

The Master's words—"Peace be with you"—needed additional

affirmation, which he provided by showing them his nail-pierced hands and the wound in his side caused by the Roman soldier's spear. He encouraged them to touch him because he knew they would then realize that a *spirit* did not have flesh and bones. Since they still had doubts, he took a piece of the broiled fish and ate it in their presence (Luke 24:40-43). He further explained that the prophetic writings in the Law of Moses, the Prophets and the Psalms pertaining to him had to be fulfilled.

Jesus Appears to Thomas

Thomas, nicknamed Didymus,—one of the original twelve apostles—was not present when Jesus visited the other disciples. They told him they had seen the Lord, touched him and watched while he ate some fish.

Then Thomas said: "Unless I see the nail marks in his hands and put my fingers where the nails were, and put my hand into his side, I will not believe it" (John 20:25). We have often heard the saying, "Seeing is believing," and that is exactly what it took to convince Thomas.

As it turned out, Thomas had an entire week to think about what the other disciples had said: "We have seen the Lord" (v.25). Could it be true, or were they simply deceived? The manner in which Jesus handled this episode provided compelling evidence. They had all gathered in the house, including Thomas, with all the doors locked. With no advanced warning, Jesus is standing among them and says: "Peace be with you" (v. 26). Before anyone had time to comment, Jesus turned to Thomas and said: "Put your finger here; see my hands. Reach out your hand and put it into my side. Stop doubting and believe" (v. 27). Thomas' response was a resounding, "My Lord and my God!" Fortunately for Thomas, the Lord was present and very anxious to perform the very deed that would restore the disciple's faith.

The apostle, John, concludes his book with this compelling thought:

> Jesus did many other miraculous signs in the presence of his disciples, which are not recorded in this book. But these are written that you may believe that Jesus is the Christ, the Son of God, and that by believing you may have life in his name (John 20:30. 31).

Evidence for the Resurrection Furnished by Enemies

The report circulated that Jesus had declared that he would be crucified, buried and in three days would rise again. The religious Pharisees were determined not to allow such a humiliating event to occur. Consequently, the chief priests and Pharisees went to Pilot and requested a guard be provided to make the tomb secure for three days. Pilate agreed with the words: "Go make the tomb as sure as you know how" (Matthew 27:65). Perhaps the governor's remarks causes one to wonder if he had doubts about their ability to secure the tomb. The soldiers secured the tomb, placed the Governor's seal on the stone and posted the guard.

The moment the women left the tomb, some of the guards hurriedly went into the city and reported to the chief priests everything that had happened. The chief priests summoned the elders and together they settled on a plan. They gave the soldiers a large sum of money and instructed them in what to say: Tell them, "his disciples came during the night and stole him away while we were asleep" (Matthew 28:13). The religious leaders further agreed that, if their explanation were reported to the governor, they would do whatever was necessary to keep the guards out of trouble. Matthew concludes: "And this story has been widely circulated among the Jews to this very day" (v. 15b).

The soldier's report was truly flimsy, but evidently it worked, since no one was held responsible for Jesus' "body" being removed from the tomb. Under normal circumstances the guards would have been brutally beaten and killed for failing to do their duty. This story serves to support what the apostles and other disciples declared in the gospels, Matthew, Mark, Luke and John that, "he is risen." Remember the words of the angel to the women:

He is not here; he has risen, just as he said. Come and see the place where he lay. Then go quickly and tell his disciples: 'He has risen from the dead and is going ahead of you into Galilee. There you will see him' (Matthew 28:5-7).

The Giving of the Great Commission

It is essential to understand that the reason Jesus left heaven and came to the earth as a human being was to provide for our deliverance from sin and to assure our salvation. This includes participating in a new way of living that can only be obtained by becoming a new creation in Christ Jesus. The old nature with its sinful desires must be crucified. In its place, Jesus Christ becomes the Lord of our lives.

When Jesus met with his disciples in Galilee following his resurrection, he explained in detail how the human race was to be reached with the gospel story. Mark recorded it with these words: "Go into all the world and preach the good news to all creation. Whoever believes and is baptized will be saved, but whoever does not believe will be condemned" (Mark 16:15, 16).

The *good news* includes the complete story of Jesus Christ as it has been covered in the previous pages of this book and found in the gospel records of Matthew, Mark, Luke and John. It is essential for a person to believe it, and to obey it.

So that no one misunderstood the gospel story, Jesus had the apostle John record exactly what was included: to Nicodemus, a member of the Jewish ruling council, Jesus declared, "I tell you the truth, no one can enter the kingdom of God unless he is born again" (John 3:3). Nicodemus was confused by Jesus' statement, for he responded by asking how someone his age could enter a second time into his mother's wound and be born again. Jesus' explanation: '"I tell you the truth, no one can enter the kingdom of God unless he is born of water and the Spirit'" (v.5).

Nicodemus was familiar with people being baptized in water, so he obviously understood that point, but to be "born of the Spirit" was a subject about which he needed help. The NIV translation of verse six, "Flesh gives birth to flesh, but the Spirit gives birth to spirit" may express the idea correctly, but the translation is awkward. A more accurate translation is: "That which is born of the flesh is flesh, and that which is born of the Spirit is spirit" (NASV). Nicodemus probably was able to comprehend from the concept that Jesus was addressing a spiritual matter, and not a physical one.

Nicodemus would have had a better understanding of Jesus' teaching if Matthew and Mark's accounts of the Great Commission had been accessible to him. Matthew records that the eleven disciples went to the mountain in Galilee—as they had been instructed—where Jesus declared:

> All authority in heaven and on earth has been given to me. Therefore go and make disciples of all nations, baptizing them in the name of the Father and of the Son and of the Holy Spirit, and teaching them to obey everything I have commanded you. And surely I am with you always, to the very end of the age (Matthew 28:18-20).

It was important for Nicodemus and people everywhere to understand that Jesus had received authority from the Father for his followers to teach and make disciples of all nations. Assurance was given that he would be with them always until the end of the age. Peter and the apostles proclaimed this Good News in Jerusalem on the day of Pentecost as recorded in Acts, chapter two. From that Pentecost day forward until time is no more, Christians will be found proclaiming Jesus Christ as humanity's Savior and Redeemer.

One point in Mark's recording of the Great Commission may need clarification. He stated that the believer who is baptized will be saved.

Question: Saved from what?

Answer: The baptized believer will be saved from sin, condemnation and spiritual death. Paul addresses this thought in writing to the church at Rome by proclaiming,

> Therefore, there is now no condemnation for those who are in Christ Jesus, because through Christ Jesus the law of the Spirit of life set me free from the law of sin and death (Romans 8:1, 2).

To the church at Corinth, he wrote that anyone "in Christ" is a new creation, "the old has gone, the new has come" (2 Corinthians 5:17). The individual "in Christ" is assured freedom from sin and death and ultimately, eternal life.

The Gospels Close—The Kingdom Anticipated

When the gospel accounts concluded, the apostles and disciples were still waiting for the kingdom to appear. Jesus told these men that the kingdom would come "with power" during their lifetime. The word "power" in the Greek text is dunamis, which implies miraculous power.

Luke opens the book of Acts by reminding Theophilus that he had recorded in his previous book events covering the life and teachings of Jesus up to the point that he was taken up to heaven. During the forty days following his resurrection, the Lord appeared to the apostles providing them with instruction regarding "the kingdom of God" (Acts 1:3). Their question was: "Lord, are you at this time going to restore the kingdom to Israel?" (v.6). The apostles obviously were thinking of the kingdom that had existed under David. They were anticipating that Jesus would restore the type of earthly kingdom over which King David had reigned.

The exchange that took place between Jesus and Pilate obviously had escaped their memory. When asked by Pilate: "Are you the king of the Jews?" Jesus replied: "My kingdom is not of this world, if it were, my servants would fight to prevent my arrest by the Jews. But now my kingdom is from another place" (John 18:33, 36). They were thinking of a physical kingdom while Jesus was addressing a spiritual dimension. Unfortunately, they did not understand the true nature of the kingdom and were still expecting Jesus to establish *his* kingdom in Jerusalem and to reign from there.

Jesus Returns to the Father in Heaven

In the next scene described by Luke, the disciples were present as Jesus suddenly was lifted up to heaven "and a cloud hid him from their sight" (Acts 1:9). Then two men in white clothing approached the disciples and assured them that, "This same Jesus, who has been taken from you into heaven, will come back in the same way you have seen him go into heaven" (v.11). As instructed, the disciples remained together in Jerusalem waiting for the Holy Spirit to come upon them.

In preparation for his departure, Jesus had given the twelve apostles their commission, namely, to take his message of salvation to the entire world as recorded in Matthew 28:18-20 and Mark 16:15, 16. Before being taken up to heaven in a cloud that hid him from their sight, Jesus' words rang out: "But you will receive power when the Holy Spirit comes on you; and you will be my witnesses in Jerusalem and in all Judea and Samaria, and to the ends of the earth" (Acts 1:8). Suddenly, they realized that Jesus was no longer present with them, so they returned to Jerusalem to the room where they had been staying. There they continued in prayer with a few disciples, expecting additional instruction to follow. While waiting, they arranged to choose a man from among them to replace Judas, who had gone to his grave. Matthias was selected, since he possessed all of the qualifications necessary to fill the role occupied by Judas.

Summary

The enemies of Jesus offered Judas money to betray his master. Jesus announced the traitor's plan to all the disciples at the evening meal. When Satan entered Judas, the Lord told him to make haste with his plan.

Jesus knew that it would devastate the apostles when he broke the news to them about his return to the Father in heaven.

To alleviate their grief, he explained that the Holy Spirit would be sent to comfort, assure accuracy and truthfulness in what they taught. In this way the world would be convicted of sin, righteousness and the judgment to come.

The women were the first to visit the tomb. They were greeted by an angel who told them to go tell the other disciples that the tomb was empty and Jesus would meet them in Galilee. At that moment Jesus stood before them, and they fell down to worship him.

Peter and John visited the tomb only to find Jesus was not there. As promised, Jesus met the disciples in Galilee but Thomas was not present. When told that they had seen the Lord, Thomas was doubtful and

> only believed after the Lord had entered the room and had him place his hands on the nail prints and also into his side. Tomas' response was, "My Lord and my God."
>
> When the book of Acts opens, Jesus is suddenly lifted up to heaven and the disciples return to Jerusalem. While waiting for further instruction, they chose Matthias to fill the vacancy left by Judas.

Chapter seven begins with Daniel's prophecy of the kingdom, demonstrating its superiority to all previous kingdoms and assuring its eternal nature.

Section Two

The Kingdom And The Church

The Kingdom That Will Never Be Destroyed

God used the prophet Daniel to explain to Nebuchadnezzar, king of Babylon, the meaning of his dream that no man could interpret.

The king asked Daniel, "Are you able to tell me what I saw in my dream and interpret it?" 'Daniel replied, "No wise man, enchanter, magician or diviner can explain to the king the mystery...but ***there is a God in heaven who reveals mysteries.*** He has shown King Nebuchadnezzar what will happen in days to come'" (Daniel 2:26-28).

"What is impossible with men is possible with God" Luke 18:27).

Chapter 7

The Prophecy of Daniel Regarding the Kingdom

Centuries before Jesus came preaching, "Repent, for the kingdom of heaven is near," the prophet Daniel wrote extensively of a kingdom that God, the Creator of the heavens and the earth, would establish. The prophet foretold that *four earthly kingdoms would rise and fall before the beginning of a kingdom established by the God of heaven.* That kingdom, Daniel declared, "will never be destroyed, and that kingdom...will crush and put an end to all these kingdoms, but it will itself *endure forever"* (Daniel 2:44, emphasis added).

Daniel's prophecy was spoken to Nebuchadnezzar, king of Babylon, who had a dream that confused and troubled him. He called in the wise men, magicians, conjurers and diviners to interpret the dream, but he refused to relate the dream's contents to them. Because they could not tell the king the contents and interpretation of the dream, Nebuchadnezzar was "furious and gave orders to destroy all the wise men of Babylon" (Daniel 2:12).

Daniel came to the rescue and convinced the king that the God of heaven would give him an answer. Arioch, the king's attendant took Daniel before the king. When asked if he could make known the dream and its interpretation, Daniel replied:

> As for the mystery about which the king has inquired, neither wise men, conjurers, magicians, nor diviners are able to declare it to the king. However, there is a God in heaven who reveals mysteries, and *He has made known to King Nebuchadnezzar what will take place in the latter days.* This was your dream and the visions in your mind while on your bed (Daniel 2:27-28, NASV, emphasis added).

At that point, Daniel explained the dream and its interpretation, which included four kingdoms.

- First kingdom: Babylonian Empire, over which Nebuchadnezzar reigned.
- Second kingdom: Medes and the Persians.
- Third kingdom: Alexandrian Empire.
- Fourth kingdom: Roman Empire.

King Nebuchadnezzar was informed that he would be driven away from people and would live with the wild animals "until you acknowledge that the Most High is sovereign over the kingdoms of men and gives them to anyone he wishes" (4:32).

Numerous details of these empires are found in Daniel 2:36-43. Beginning with verse 44, the prophet explained that,

> in the days of those kings the God of heaven will set up a kingdom which will never be destroyed, and that kingdom will not be left for another people; it will crush and put an end to all these kingdoms, but it will itself endure forever.

This prophecy of an everlasting, divinely established kingdom was fulfilled by Jesus, when He said: "Repent, for the kingdom of heaven is near" (Matthew 4:17). It is the same kingdom Luke writes about in Acts, chapter two that had its beginning in A.D. 33 on the Day of Pentecost in the city of Jerusalem.

Fulfillment of Daniel's Prophecy

Early in the gospel of Matthew, he has both John the Baptizer and Jesus beginning their ministry with the statement, "Repent, for the kingdom of heaven is near" (Matthew 3:2; 4:17). Of the 54 times Matthew refers to the kingdom, only five are designated "kingdom of God." Mark, Luke and John, on the other hand, use "kingdom of God" exclusively. If Matthew intended to make a distinction, the passages where *kingdom of God* appears are not helpful in arriving at the difference.

Near the beginning of his public ministry, Jesus used a variety of approaches to describe the nature of the kingdom. For example, Mark records Jesus asking, "What shall we say the kingdom of God is like?" (Mark 4:30). Luke, on the other hand, records, "What shall I compare it to?" (Luke 13:18). Matthew (chapter 13) reports Jesus comparing the kingdom to a variety of subjects and substances: mustard seed, weeds, yeast, a fish net, a land owner, the owner of a house and a merchant looking for fine pearls. In each comparison, Jesus was showing how things began in a very small way but grew into something large. In most cases, the expansion was fruitful and valuable. Out of the many comparisons with the kingdom cited, only two will be examined—the mustard seed and weeds.

The Mustard Seed

Mustard seed is one of the smallest seeds found in a garden, but when planted, it will sprout and mature into a large plant where the birds can rest while being protected from the hot sun or undesirable weather. In a similar way, the kingdom of heaven began with few people but grew to where it covered the known world.

Parable of the Weeds

In the parable of the weeds, Jesus compared the kingdom of heaven to a farmer who sowed good seed in his field. Without warning an enemy also sowed weeds in the farmer's field. When the wheat sprouted, so did the weeds.

The servants reported this terrible event to the owner, asking him what should be done. They were ready to go pull up the weeds, but the wise owner ordered his servants to let both grow until harvest time so as not to disturb the roots of the wheat and hinder its growth. At the time of harvesting, the workers would collect the weeds in bundles and burn them. Afterward, the wheat would be gathered and stored in barns.

Jesus explained this parable to his disciples, identifying its various components (Matthew 13: 37-39):

- The one who sowed the good seed is the Son of Man.
- The field is the world.
- The good seed stands for the sons of the kingdom.
- The weeds are the sons of the evil one.
- The enemy who sows the weeds is the devil.
- The harvest is the end of the age.
- The harvesters are angels.

Other Scriptures help in further clarifying the parable:

- The Son of Man is Jesus Christ, whom John in Revelation identifies as "King of kings and Lord of lords" (Revelation 19:16).
- The good seed is "the word of God"(Luke 8:11).

- o The field is "the world" where the sons and daughters of the kingdom reside, or live (Mark 16:15).
- o The weeds are sons of the evil one sown by the enemy, who is the devil (Matthew 13:38).

Jesus described in detail the events that will occur when the Son of Man comes in his glory with all of his angels (Matthew 25:31-34, 41, 46):

> he will separate the people one from another as a shepherd separates the sheep from the goats. He will put the sheep on his right and the goats on his left. "Then the King will say to those on his right, '...take your inheritance, the kingdom prepared for you since the creation of the world.'
>
> "Then he will say to those on his left, 'Depart from me, you who are cursed, into the eternal fire prepared for the devil and his angels.'"
>
> 'Then they will go away to eternal punishment, but the righteous to eternal life."

It is important to observe that in making the comparisons regarding the kingdom, Jesus used examples that describe both good and evil. The final result is the consequence of choices made by each person.

Choosing Twelve Apostles

When Jesus chose and commissioned the twelve disciples, Luke writes: "He sent them out to proclaim the kingdom of God" (Luke 9:2). In teaching them about prayer, he said: "Pray, then in this way...

Thy kingdom come" (Matthew 6:9, 10, NASV). From this remark, we can conclude that at this time the kingdom is yet to be established. In Matthew 13, Jesus described the kingdom by using eight parables. His comparisons evoked scenes that the audience would recognize and could understand.

Jesus admonished his disciples to put God first, as he taught them about priorities in their lives and keeping things in order. Two examples of "prioritizing" in their lives were:

- They could not serve two masters. (Matthew 6:24).
- They should not be anxious about food and clothing, 'What shall we eat?' or 'What shall we drink?' or 'What shall we wear?'" They should trust the heavenly Father to provide these needs. But seek first his kingdom and his righteousness; and all these things will be given to you as well (Matthew 6:30-33).

When to Expect the Kingdom?

At what point would the kingdom be explained and its appearance declared? Following his *Sermon on the Mount* (Matthew chapters 5-7), Jesus traveled to all the cities and villages teaching in their synagogues and proclaiming the gospel of the kingdom. He continued to heal various kinds of diseases and sicknesses.

Matthew further explains in chapter ten that Jesus chose twelve apostles and identified them by name. They were given instructions indicating their mission would lead them to "the lost sheep of Israel" (Matthew 10:6).

The beginning point of their message was, "The kingdom of heaven is near" (v.7). It appears from this statement that the kingdom was soon to appear. Jesus gave a time line of when to expect the kingdom. He declared that some of his listeners standing there would not die without seeing "the kingdom of God come with power"

(Mark 9:1). This statement restricts the coming of the kingdom to the lifetime of some of his disciples.

Luke also records two passages indicating the timing for the coming of the kingdom.

First, Luke describes a confrontation between Jesus and the Pharisees, who ask when they could expect the kingdom of God. Jesus replied, "The kingdom of God does not come with your careful observation, nor will people say, 'Here it is,' or 'There it is,' because the kingdom of God is within you" (Luke 17:20-21). Interpretation of these verses hinges on translation of the Greek word ἐντὸς, (entos). Four translations (New International Version, King James Version, American Standard Version, Confraternity) translate it "within," while the Revised Standard Version renders it "in the midst," the New American Standard Version "in your midst," and some versions prefer "among." Which translation is more accurate? It comes down to the meaning of the word entos, (Gk, ἐντὸς). While some scholars take it to be an adverb of place, most translate it as "in" or "within."

Second, Luke 18:15-17 describes the occasion of children being brought to Jesus, who says: "Let the children come to me, and do not hinder them: for the kingdom of God belongs to such as these." Jesus continued: "anyone who does not receive the kingdom of God like a child will never enter it." This passage raises a question regarding the kingdom being "within" us. The passage appears to be teaching that to enter the kingdom one's attitude must be comparable to that of a child.

In light of the apostle John's teaching in the book of Revelation 11:15, where he writes, "'The kingdom of the world has become the kingdom of our Lord and of his Christ, and he will reign forever and ever,"' it seems likely that the meaning could be taken either way depending on the context of the passages cited.

Passages Implying the Kingdom Already Existed

Throughout the Sermon on the Mount, Jesus made comments

regarding the kingdom, leaving the thought that it already existed. For example, in Matthew 5:3, he referred to the poor in spirit and added, "for theirs *is* the kingdom of heaven." In verse 10, talking about those persecuted for righteousness sake, he stated, "for theirs *is* the kingdom of heaven." In commenting about John the Baptist, Jesus' statement follows: "he who *is* least in the kingdom of heaven *is* greater than he" (Matthew 11:11; Luke 7:28). In Matthew 19:23, Jesus commented: "It *is* hard for a rich man to enter the kingdom of heaven." (Additional passages could be consulted: Matthew 13:24, 31, 44, 47; 18:1, 29.) The verb "is" in these and many other passages is present tense, leaving the impression that the kingdom is already in existence.

One additional verse: "Jesus said to them, "'I tell you the truth, the tax collectors and the prostitutes *are* entering the kingdom of God ahead of you'" (Matthew 21:31). Again, the verb "are" is present tense, not future.

It is clear that the kingdom is in the process of being formed and may explain this usage.

Teaching That Contradicts the Gospel Accounts

A number of religious groups teach that Jesus came intending to establish a kingdom, but was unable to complete his mission because the people rejected him.

Consequently, he turned to a substitute plan, which meant establishing the church. The problem with this conclusion is its failure to accept inspired statements made by Gospel writers, especially Mark 9:1, which records Jesus' declaration that some people in the audience would still be living when the kingdom came with power. In addition, Matthew 16:28 and Luke 9:27 teach that the kingdom would (a) appear during the lifetime of some of these disciples and (b) be recognizable by the power that accompanied it. Since all of the men in Jesus' generation died within the period of a few years, the kingdom would have had to appear soon.

Additional evidence appears on the occasion when Jesus was observing the Passover feast with his disciples. During the meal he instituted the Lord's Supper. After serving the bread and the fruit of the vine, he gave thanks, adding that he would "not drink of this fruit of the vine...until that day when I drink it new with you in My Father's kingdom" (Matthew 26:29, NASV). His statement was a reference to the time when the kingdom, also designated the church, would begin in Jerusalem as recorded in Acts, chapter 2. Luke and Paul use the terms *kingdom* and *church* throughout the Book of Acts while also mentioning their participation in the Lord's Supper (Acts 20:7-11). It is clear, beginning with the Book of Acts that the kingdom is now in existence, and the Lord communes with Christians each time we come together to partake of the Lord's Supper.

All of the facts presented by the above Scriptures establish a difficulty in accepting the teaching that Jesus failed in establishing his kingdom and reluctantly turned to building his church instead. If he failed in establishing his kingdom, what reason is there to believe that a plan to establish the church would be successful? This argument creates too much uncertainty and is totally unacceptable. Scripture truths reveal that Jesus accomplished exactly what he planned. The kingdom of heaven was ushered in during the lifetime of some of his disciples.

It is clear from both Mark and Luke's gospel accounts that the disciples were looking for the kingdom to appear at Christ's crucifixion. Mark wrote that Joseph of Arimathea was "waiting for the kingdom of God" when Jesus was crucified. Joseph was courageous enough to appear before Pilate and ask for his body. After checking with the centurion to determine whether or not Jesus was dead, Pilate allowed the body to be turned over to Joseph, who prepared it for a respectable burial and placed it in a tomb hewn out in the rock (Mark 15: 42-45; Luke 23:50-53).

Following his resurrection from the tomb, Jesus spent the next forty days, (Acts 1:3b), talking about the kingdom of God and opening the minds of the apostles "so they could understand the Scriptures"

(Luke 24:45). He added that "repentance and forgiveness of sins" was to "be preached in his name to all nations, beginning at Jerusalem. You are witnesses of these things" (Luke 24:46-48). They were admonished to remain in Jerusalem until they were "clothed with power from on high" (v.49).

The Book of Acts opens with Luke elaborating on the above thoughts promised by the Father, how that within a few days the apostles would "be baptized with the Holy Spirit" (Acts 1:5). This affirmed their commitment to become his "witnesses in Jerusalem, and in all Judaea and Samaria, and to the ends of the earth" (Acts 1:8).

While they were present, the Lord was lifted up into the heavens "before their very eyes, and a cloud hid him from their sight" (v.9). With this, his mission on earth was complete, and the development of the kingdom and church was handed over to the apostles with their assignment beginning in Jerusalem on the day of Pentecost (Acts 2).

Summary

The Lord used the prophet Daniel to describe the nature of the kingdom over which Jesus would rule and reign once he began his public ministry.

In the same way Jesus brought clarity to teaching regarding other subjects, he used parables and comparisons to explain the nature of the kingdom.

In Matthew's gospel, Jesus began his ministry, saying: "Repent, for the kingdom of heaven is near" (4:17).

Luke has Jesus declaring he was sent to preach the good news of the kingdom of God (4:43).

> In Mark 9:1 Jesus declared the kingdom would come during the lifetime of some of the disciples. Matthew and Luke record similar accounts in (Mathew 16:28; Luke 9:27).
>
> Following his resurrection, Jesus spent the next 40 days teaching about the kingdom of God, and equipping the apostles regarding their future mission.
>
> The Book of Acts opens referring to the Father's promise that the apostles would "be baptized with the Holy Spirit" (1:5). This would equip them to be the Lord's "witnesses in Jerusalem...Judaea,... Samaria, and to the ends of the earth" (1:8).
>
> They were present when the Lord was lifted up into the heavens "before their very eyes, and a cloud hid him from their sight" (1:8).

Chapter eight begins with the Celebration of Pentecost and the apostles are all together in Jerusalem. What happens next involves a miracle that requires considerable explanation by the apostle Peter. It is also clear that Peter is the chief spokesman until the time that the Gentiles are accepted by the Lord in the same way as the Jews.

Pentecost Celebration Included Miracles

The apostles were all together in Jerusalem waiting for instruction about what they should do. Suddenly the room where they were meeting "was filled with a violent wind and tongues of fire came down from heaven and were resting upon them. They were all filled with the Holy Spirit and began to speak in languages unknown to them (Acts 2:1-8).

The multitude was amazed and perplexed because they knew these men were Galileans and each one was hearing them speaking in his own native language (vv. 7-11). Only a miracle could explain what was happening.

Never Forget What Jesus Said: "What is impossible with men is possible with God" (Luke 18:27).

Chapter 8

Celebration of Pentecost

It was the season for Pentecost to be celebrated and the apostles were all together in Jerusalem, as Jesus had instructed before his ascension to heaven.

Pentecost was the second of the great Jewish national festivals and was observed on the 50th day, or seven weeks from the Paschal Feast. In the Old *Testament,* it was called *the feast of weeks.* It was a festival of good cheer, a day of joy.[1]

Suddenly the place where the apostles were meeting was filled with a violent wind and tongues of fire coming down from heaven were resting upon them. Luke explains that they were all "filled with the Holy Spirit and began to speak in other tongues as the Spirit enabled them" (Acts 2:4). All twelve apostles—Matthias was chosen to replace Judas— were active in explaining this unusual event to the *crowd* of people that Luke records as coming "together in bewilderment, because each one heard them speaking in his own language" (2:6).

This crowd was large, consisting of Jews who spoke sixteen different languages and dialects. What shocked the listeners was the fact that they were able to hear and understand the message. Some in the audience were in total confusion and they accused the apostles of being drunk. Since the apostles were common, ordinary people from Galilee with no special training, the people were amazed by the events taking place.

Peter Addresses the Multitude

The apostle Peter stood up and declared that the audience was witnessing the fulfillment of Joel's prophecy of a day when the Lord would pour out His Spirit on all people. Their sons and daughters would prophesy; their old men would dream dreams; their young men would see visions, and all who called on the name of the Lord would be saved (Joel 2:28-32).

Immediately, the apostle launched into a lengthy message explaining that they were witnessing the fulfillment of the prophet's message, including God's promise to resurrect Jesus and to make him both Lord and Christ (Acts 2:14-36).

Peter's sermon stirred the listeners' emotions to the degree that they were pierced to their hearts and overwhelmed with guilt. They had just been reminded that they had put Jesus to death by "nailing him to the cross" (v. 23). Their response was a question: "Brothers, what shall we do?" Peter replied,

> Repent and be baptized every one of you, in the name of Jesus Christ for the forgiveness of your sins. And you will receive the gift of the Holy Spirit (Acts 2:38).

He assured them that the promise was for them, their children and people everywhere. He continued with a powerful message, warning and pleading with them to, "Save yourselves from this corrupt generation" (v. 40). His comment prompted an immediate response because about 3,000 people were baptized that same day.

Luke did not take time to describe the baptism scene, but one can imagine what was involved in immersing 3000 people. The largest number I have witnessed being baptized at the same time was not more than a dozen. In our case, there was always available a change of garments so the candidate could change into dry clothing afterward. Certainly, that was not true for these people. We are not told how many apostles were engaged in performing the baptisms; perhaps all twelve were involved. If so, the event would have required a huge pool of water to make room for that number to be in the pool at the same time or the use of several pools in and around Jerusalem. We can be assured that this event turned into a mighty long day.

Certainly, nothing of this magnitude had happened before among God's people, and it is highly unlikely that it will ever happen again. Perhaps we can have Peter or one of the apostles explain in detail exactly how it all took place once we join that heavenly host in the eternal realm.

It does seem reasonable to conclude that what transpired in Jerusalem on the day of Pentecost constituted the fulfillment of the kingdom prophecies, since Luke opened the book of Acts discussing how Jesus had appeared to these men over a period of more than forty days talking about the kingdom. He further instructed them not to leave Jerusalem, but to wait for the gift promised by the Father, which would include baptism with the Holy Spirit (Acts 1:3-5).

Most commentators refer to Peter's message starting in Acts 2:14 as the beginning of the church; however, nothing is said by Luke in the text to justify this thought. Later, Luke wrote in Acts 5:11 that "great fear seized the whole church" once the story began to circulate regarding the death of Ananias and Sapphira.

By now, word was spreading that a new movement was under way and people were joining in large numbers the ranks of the disciples. They were meeting daily in the temple courts to receive additional instruction from the apostles regarding their new way of life. They were breaking bread, spending time in prayer and sharing fellowship together in their homes, while "praising God and enjoying the favor of all the people" (Acts 2:47). The chapter ends on a high note: "the Lord added to their number daily those who were being saved" (v. 47b).

Events after Pentecost

The religious Pharisees and Sadducees realized they were rapidly losing control of the situation. As a result, the priests, the captain of the temple guard and the Sadducees visited Peter and John who were speaking to the people. The authorities questioned the source of the power and in what name they had healed a man "lame from his mother's womb" (Acts 3:2, NASV). Adding insult to injury for the religious leaders, about 5,000 people, who heard Peter and John speak, accepted the gospel message and joined their ranks that day (Acts 4:4).

In hopes of putting an end to the movement, the religious leaders arrested Peter and John and put them in jail. The following day, Peter and John were brought out of the jail to be interrogated. When asked by what power and in whose name they were doing this, the apostle Peter, filled with the Holy Spirit, answered:

> Rulers and elders of the people! If we are being called to account today for an act of kindness shown to a cripple and are asked how he was healed, then know this, you and all the people of Israel: It is by the name of Jesus Christ of Nazareth, whom you crucified but whom God raised from the dead, that this man stands before you healed! (Acts 4:8-10).

Since the man who had been a cripple was standing before them, the critics were silenced with nothing more to say. Peter concluded the meeting with the statement that "Salvation is found in no one else, for there is no other name under heaven given to men by which we must be saved" (Acts 4:12). Peter and John's courage astounded the religious leaders because they recognized them to be ordinary men with little formal training. These leaders were unable to dismiss the realization that "these men had been with Jesus" (Acts 4:13). Until that moment, they were only focused on the apostles and their teaching. Those—unlike the multitudes—who responded in baptism were added to the number of the believers and apostles who were being saved (Acts 2:47).

The Believers Share Their Possessions

Many of the people had traveled considerable distance to gather in Jerusalem to celebrate this festival. They obviously had no intention of staying longer once that event ended. To provide for the huge crowds, the people were sharing their possessions even to the point of selling property and bringing the proceeds to the apostles for distribution wherever there was a need. Luke tells about Joseph, a Levite from Cyprus, who sold a field and brought the money to the apostles. Joseph's example inspired Ananias and his wife, Sapphira, to sell a piece of property. However, the manner in which this transaction was handled led to their death. When questioned regarding the price received for the property sold, they failed to tell the truth. Peter referred to this event as "testing the Spirit of the Lord" (Acts 5:1-11), and they fell down and died. This surely made a genuine impression on the Christians who witnessed the event.

Introduction of the Church

At the conclusion of this episode, Luke wrote: "Great fear seized the whole *church*" (Acts 5:11, emphasis added). It should be noted that the King James Version translated Acts2:47 as "the Lord added to the church" but other versions using older Greek manuscripts translate this verse as "added to them," (ASV); "added to their number," (RSV, NIV); "added to their company," (Confraternity); in place of "added to the church" (KJV). Since the KJV was translated from the *Textus Receptus*—a much later Greek text than used by the other versions—the word, (church" was likely supplied by a scribe who concluded that "church" appropriately represented the meaning.

Consequently, it is easy to be confused by these different translations of the meaning of Acts 2:47. "fear seizing the whole church." Since Luke made no mention of the church before Acts 2:47, how would the reader know to tie this concept to Jesus' statement in Matthew 16:18 that he would build his church? In fact, if one began reading in the Book of Acts without first reading Matthew's Gospel, one would have no idea as to why the church is mentioned in this context. Even the person who has read Matthew's account would still be wondering when to expect the beginning of the church. All that Jesus said in Matthew 16:18 was, "I will build my church." There is not even a hint as to when this would occur, and we have no help following Acts 5:11. It is just as though the reader should know and understand that this "church" is the spiritual body Jesus declared that he would build.

Anyone who had access to the Ephesian letter and was familiar with chapter two, possibly would have concluded that Paul was referring to the church in verses 19 through 22. There, the apostle talks about our being "fellow citizens with God's people and members of God's household, built on the foundation of the apostles and prophets, with Christ Jesus himself as the chief cornerstone" (vv. 19, 20).

The believers gathered for a prayer meeting and together they raised their voices with the words: "Sovereign Lord,... You made the heaven and the earth and the sea and everything in them" (Acts 4:24). They continued pleading for God to answer their petition and enable them to speak the word with great boldness. When the prayer ended, "the place where they were meeting was shaken. And they were all filled with the Holy Spirit and spoke the word of God boldly" (v. 31).

Development of the Church in the New Testament

The ministry of Jesus, up to the previous account involving Ananias and Sapphira, was focused on *the kingdom*. Following that event, attention is shifted to the *church,* with only occasional reference to the kingdom.

To obtain a more detailed picture of the *church,* we need to return to the Gospel of Matthew, chapter sixteen. There, Jesus is involved in conversation with his disciples regarding his identity. They had just entered the district of Caesarea, Philippi when Jesus raised a question focused on what people were saying about him. Their answer was that some were confusing him with John the Baptist while others were associating him with Jeremiah or one of the prophets. Without delay, he put the question straight to them: "Who do you say I am?" (Matthew 16:15). Peter, who seldom wasted time in coming up with a response, replied: "You are the Christ, the Son of the living God" (v. 16). The Lord was quick to point out that Peter's answer did not originate from the thinking of any person but from God Himself. He continued: "And I tell you that you are Peter, and on this rock I will build my church, and the gates of Hades will not overcome it" (v. 18).

We assume that these men knew nothing about the church prior to this conversation. No record exists in the Scriptures or secular history that implies the contrary. What is clear in this conversation is that Jesus intended to build his church at some point in the future because he used the future verb tense—"I will build." As stated earlier, no help is given in this conversation as to when this would take place. It does, however, carry the certainty that the gates of Hades could not prevent it nor overcome it. This was Jesus' way of declaring that his church would be so powerful that Satan's best defense would not be able to keep it out of any place on earth.

Mistaken Identity Attributed to Peter

Roman Catholic theologians have taken Jesus' statement regarding "the rock" to be referring to Peter. If this was true, the church would have its foundation on Peter, but a problem immediately exists with this interpretation. When Jesus referred to "Peter," he used a masculine gender Greek word, Πέτρος (petros) meaning "a stone, a rock, a detached but large fragment."[2] When the Lord said, "Upon this rock, (*petra*) I will build my church," he was referring to the distinction used in classical Greek where ταύτῃ τῇ πέτρᾳ (*petra*) means "the massive living rock."[3] With this distinction, it is clear that Jesus was not implying that Peter was the rock upon which his *ekklesia* (church) would be built, but on the statement of confession that he is the Son of God.

The above distinction is not necessary for one to conclude that this teaching is inaccurate. Peter's life was everything but a firm foundation. During this episode Jesus rebuked Peter by saying: "Get behind me Satan! You are a stumbling block to me; you do not have in mind the things of God but the things of men" (Matthew 16:22-23). Add to this the occasion when Jesus was before the Sanhedrin being questioned by the High Priest, Caiaphas. The apostle denied knowing the Lord three times, just as the Master had said he would do (Matthew 26:69-75).

The following event took place while Paul and Barnabas were working with the church in Antioch. The rapid growth prompted Peter to stop by for a visit. While he was there, the apostle Paul was compelled to describe his visit and the confrontation that ensued:

> When Peter came to Antioch, I opposed him to his face, because he was clearly in the wrong. Before certain men came from James, he used to eat with the Gentiles. But when they arrived, he began to draw back and separate himself from the Gentiles

> because he was afraid of those who belonged to the circumcision group (Galatians 2:11-12).

The Lord's church obviously possessed a more permanent foundation than Peter's life. Jesus sealed the thought when he said concerning the church he would build: "the gates of Hades will not overcome it" (Matthew 16:18).

The word *katiscuo,* (Gk κατισχύσουσιν (translated "overcome") means "to be strong, powerful, gain the ascendency, be dominant, prevail, win a victory over."[4] The idea is that nothing can overpower the church that Jesus built. So, regardless of the interpretation assigned to the words *petra* and *petros,* it is unacceptable to maintain that the church is built on Peter.

Jesus referred to the church during his public ministry only one other time In the gospel accounts when he gave instructions on solving personal differences. A disagreement or dispute that cannot be settled between individuals or with witnesses present—the Lord stated is to be to be taken "before the church" (Matthew 18:17). Read the entire context if you have a question about how problems are to be handled. The next reference to the church appears in Acts 5:11 unless the appearance of the word "church" in Acts 2:47 of the KJV is accepted as being authentic.

What is most significant in these two examples is that reference to the kingdom is also discussed in both. In Matthew chapter sixteen, Jesus is quoted as saying to Peter immediately following his reference to the church: "I will give you the keys of the kingdom of heaven; whatever you bind on earth will be bound in heaven, and whatever you loose on earth will be loosed in heaven" (v. 19). In chapter eighteen, the conversation was dealing with who was greatest in the kingdom of heaven. The thought of binding and loosing that was spoken to Peter in chapter 16 is repeated in chapter eighteen, verse 18, and applies to all of the apostles, not just to Peter.

The fact that both *kingdom* and *church* appear together in the same context causes one to conclude that they are one and the same.

What we do know is that from Matthew chapter eighteen and forward, whatever Jesus did during his earthly ministry was related to kingdom business.

Getting back to the time where Luke first mentioned that "great fear seized the whole church" following the death of Ananias and Sapphira in Acts 5:11, the apostles are found doing many miraculous signs, such as healing the sick, including those tormented by evil spirits. As word of the apostles' activities spread, large crowds of men and women came from towns around Jerusalem believing in the Lord and being added to their numbers (Acts 5:12-16).

The Apostles Arrested and Put in Jail

As expected, the high priest and members of the party of the Sadducees grew extremely jealous of the church's growth to the point that they arrested and jailed the apostles. Their intent was to bring them before the fully assembled Sanhedrin the following day (Acts 5:17-24). However, the officers, who were sent to bring them out, returned saying: "We found the jail securely locked, with the guards standing at the doors; but when we opened them, we found no one inside" (v. 23). Then, a report came saying that these men were in the temple courts telling the people the full message of this new way of life (v. 20).

The temple guard and his officers were sent to bring them out, but they did not use force because they were afraid the people would stone them. When assembled, the high priest reminded the apostles that they had been given strict orders not to teach in the name of Jesus. Peter and the other apostles responded: "We must obey God rather than men" (v. 29). This response angered the chief priests to the point that they wanted to kill them, but a wise Pharisee named Gamaliel warned that this could prove to be a genuine mistake. His advice prevailed, and the apostles were flogged and released. They departed the Sanhedrin "rejoicing because they had been counted worthy of suffering disgrace for the Name" (v. 41). Luke's use of "the Name" was his inspired way of identifying the followers of Jesus Christ. At this point, clearly, a new movement had developed in Jerusalem which was focused around the apostles and labeled the *church,* with men preaching "good news of the kingdom of God and the name of Jesus Christ" (Acts 8:12).

Any question regarding when the church began, was settled by the apostle Paul's letter to the Ephesian church. In chapter two, he described how God reconciled both Jew and Greek to Himself through the cross of Christ. In this way, both groups gained access to the Father by the one Spirit.

> Consequently, the Gentiles are no longer foreigners and aliens, but fellow citizens with God's people and members of God's household, built on the foundation of the apostles and prophets, with Christ Jesus himself as the chief cornerstone. In him the whole building is joined together and rises to become a holy temple in the Lord (Ephesians 2:19-21).

Paul's use of the expression, "members of God's household, built on the foundation of the apostles and prophets, with Christ Jesus as the chief cornerstone," is definitely a reference to the church that began on Pentecost, A.D. 33. Add to this, his comment in1Timothy 3:15, where he calls *God's household* "the church of the living God." Therefore, the matter is settled: the church and the kingdom are the same.

Christians Persecuted in Jerusalem

Following the stoning of Stephen recorded in Acts, chapter seven, "a great persecution broke out against the *church* at Jerusalem, and all except the apostles were scattered throughout Judea and Samaria" (Acts 8:1, emphasis added).

Within this time frame, Luke introduces Saul of Tarsus, who had the good fortune of being able to leave home as a young man and go to Jerusalem where he received much of his education under the great teacher of the Law, Gamaliel. While in Jerusalem, Saul (Paul) developed an understanding about Christians that convinced him to oppose the church with extreme measures. Consequently, he went from house to house arresting and throwing into jail anyone sympathetic to the Christian cause. The only positive thing that can be said regarding Paul's conduct, at this time, was his later claim to have persecuted the church "with a perfectly good conscience" (Acts 23:1, NASV). In other words, he believed that it was the right thing to do. Little did he know that the Lord was grooming him to become an apostle of Christ Jesus to the Gentiles.

Luke records the events surrounding Saul's journey to Damascus with letters from the high priest in Jerusalem to locate and arrest both men and women who were converts to Christianity. During this journey, the Lord surrounded him with a bright light and spoke to him, saying,: "Saul, Saul, why do you persecute me?" (Acts 9:4), The light blinded him, and he had to be led into Damascus. Three days later, the Lord sent Ananias to him, who explained what he needed to do to be saved (Acts 22:12-18).

This experience brought about a complete reversal of his intentions. Immediately, he began to "preach in the synagogues that Jesus is the Son of God" (Acts 9:20). The listeners knew that this man had raised havoc in Jerusalem among the disciples. Therefore, it is no surprise that the people were baffled with Saul's sudden turnaround.

After several days, word got out that the Jews intended to kill Saul. Consequently, his followers took him by night and lowered him in a basket through an opening in the wall (9:25). He hurriedly made his way to Jerusalem only to find that the disciples there, were also afraid of him. Fortunately for Saul, a disciple named Barnabas stepped forward and introduced him to the apostles. It happened that Barnabas was sufficiently familiar with Saul's case that he was able to convince the apostles that the Lord had spoken to Saul in Damascus and afterward he had preached fearlessly in the name of the Lord (9:28).

All went well until Saul's conversation with the Grecian Jews turned into debate. This debate aroused a feeling of animosity to the extent that the Jews attempted to kill Saul. When the Christians learned of this plot, they arranged for him to be sent to Tarsus. They concluded that there was no way for his safety to be assured if he remained in Jerusalem. From that event and throughout the remainder of his ministry, opposition to Paul's teaching, by an element of the Jews, was so intense that he frequently would be run out of town. Nothing, however, could discourage this dedicated soldier of Christ who was the Lord's chosen vessel to bear his "name before the Gentiles and kings and the children of Israel" (Acts 9:15).

Despite Saul's previous effort to stop the spread of Christianity, Christ was now being proclaimed and miracles were being performed wherever the disciples traveled. Philip is a good example, for he left Jerusalem and went down to Samaria. The record states that he was preaching "the good news of the kingdom of God and the name of Jesus Christ" (Acts 8:12).

Following his conversion and escape from the people in Jerusalem who wanted to kill him, Saul immediately showed up in the synagogues in Damascus, proclaiming Jesus and saying, "Jesus is the Son of God" (Acts 9:20). His preaching in Damascus began a mission that grew for years and extended all over the Mediterranean world.

Saul of Tarsus, who became Paul an apostle of Christ Jesus, impacted Christianity in a way that words are inadequate to express. The apostle's name change from Saul to Paul was appropriate, since the Lord identified him as his chosen instrument to bear his name "before the Gentiles and kings and the sons of Israel" (Acts 9:15, NASV). The name, *Saul,* originated in Judaism but *Paul* came from the Gentile race.

As Paul's ministry expanded, he placed more emphasis on the

church with fewer references to the kingdom because the apostle could appropriately identify the church as the Lord's "called out" ones. Christians were "called out" of Satan's realm; or delivered from the domain of darkness, and transferred into the kingdom of His beloved Son (Colossians 1:13, NASV). This concept of the church covered both ideas adequately.

When Paul described the "body concept," in 1 Corinthians 12, he included a new dimension of the church that was easy to understand. He wrote that the physical body has many members—eye, ears, nose, hands, feet—just as the spiritual body of Christ has many members, but *only One Head,* Christ Jesus. This comparison did not require the mind of a genius to understand. Therefore, the transition from kingdom to church and to body for purposes of clarity was—and is—especially helpful for all ages to grasp.

Next follows an expression used frequently throughout the remainder of the New Testament.

> Then the *church* throughout Judea, Galilee and Samaria enjoyed a time of peace. It was strengthened; and encouraged by the Holy Spirit, it grew in numbers, living in the fear of the Lord (Acts 9:31, emphasis added).

Since *ekklesia* refers to "the called out ones," the singular use of "church" in this passage identifies the entire number of Christians as one unit. Those residing in Judea formed one collective body as did those living in Galilee and Samaria.

Peters' Vision Prepared the Jews to Accept Gentiles

While Peter was traveling about the country, he stopped in Joppa where he spent some time with Simon the tanner. While there, Cornelius, a Roman soldier in charge of an Italian Regiment, had a vision in which an angel of God appeared and told him to send to Joppa and bring back Peter, who would deliver an important message to his household. At the same time the Lord prepared Peter so he would be willing to go with the soldiers once they located where he was staying. Peter was on the housetop praying when the angel commanding him to "rise, kill and eat" an assortment of animals, reptiles, and birds appearing on a descending sheet that Peter knew was unclean and forbidden by the Law of Moses. Peter objected to the command: "Surely not, Lord!...I have never eaten anything impure or unclean" (Acts 10:13, 14). The voice spoke to him a second time, "Do not call anything impure that God has made clean" (v.15). The vision was repeated three times.

When Cornelius' men arrived and announced their reason for coming, Peter immediately accompanied them, convinced that the vision was God's way of telling him something very important was about to happen. Upon Peter's arrival, Cornelius had assembled his relatives and close friends to listen to Peter's message. After Cornelius explained why he had sent for Peter, the apostle began to speak: "I now realize how true it is that God does not show favoritism but accepts men from every nation who fear him and do what is right" (Acts 10:34, 35). While Peter was still speaking, the Holy Spirit came on all of them in the same way he had come on the Jews. Then Peter commanded them to "be baptized in the name of Jesus Christ" (Acts 10:48).

It was necessary for Peter to explain fully to the apostles and the brothers throughout Judea what had happened that convinced him to baptize Cornelius, his household and friends. For a period of time this message still was being presented to Jews only. It took some men from Cyprus and Cyrene who visited Antioch to tell the good news about Jesus to the Gentiles. (Acts 11:19-21). These traditions and interpretations of the Law of Moses that were cherished were not quickly abandoned.

Following the persecution in Jerusalem, a number of the believers traveled north to Antioch and began to share the good news of Jesus Christ with the Gentiles. Luke writes that "The Lord's hand was with them, and a great number of people believed and turned to the Lord" (Acts 11:21).

Encouragement Brings Out the Best in People

The blessing of encouragement is seen in the life of Barnabas, who was selected by the *church* in Jerusalem to go to Antioch and encourage the new converts. The name, Barnabas, according to Acts 4:36, means (Son of Encouragement). He is described as "a good man, full of the Holy Spirit and faith" (Acts 11:24). It was in Damascus that Barnabas learned about Saul and his conversion.

Following the apostle Peter's experience, recorded in Acts chapters ten and eleven, it became clear to Peter that the Lord was accepting the Gentiles into the church. As a result disciples traveled to Antioch telling the good news about the Lord Jesus to the Gentiles. Consequently, great numbers of people believed and turned to the Lord (Acts 11:19-21). Once the church in Jerusalem became aware of these developments, they arranged to send Barnabas to Antioch. Upon arrival, Barnabas observed "the evidence of the grace of God" (v. 23) and began encouraging the disciples "to remain true to the Lord with all their hearts" (v. 23).

Rapid Growth in Antioch Required Help

The growth of the church in Antioch was expanding so rapidly that Barnabas felt compelled to get help, and he turned to Paul for assistance. He traveled to Tarsus, Saul's hometown, located Saul and talked him into returning to Damascus. Luke explains: "So for a whole year Barnabas and Saul met with the church and taught great numbers of people" (Acts 11:26). The religious world today might never have heard of Paul, the great apostle to the Gentiles, had it not been for Barnabas. He convinced the disciples that the apostle was sincerely genuine following his conversion and could be trusted.

Barnabas introduced Paul to the apostles in Jerusalem and convinced the church that he truly had turned to the Lord. So Barnabas went looking for Paul when he needed help in Antioch of Syria.

As the two men worked together in the church, a change occurred in Luke's reporting of their names: In Acts 11:26, Luke wrote: "So for a whole year Barnabas and Saul met with the church and taught great numbers of people." But in Acts 13:42, 43, 46, the order in which their names appear changes from "Barnabas and Paul" to "Paul and Barnabas." Paul obviously had the greater leadership ability and was personally called by the Lord himself. But it was Barnabas, the encourager, who first stood up for Paul, while he was still known as Saul to everyone.

The lesson for the church today: We need more people like Barnabas who receive genuine satisfaction from being encouragers without caring who gets the credit. Churches fortunate enough to be blessed with a few members of the caliber of Barnabas are destined to grow spiritually and numerically. We must not underestimate the good being done by encouraging others. One result might be discovering another Paul. Remember, as a result of the efforts of these two men, the church at Antioch had the distinction of being the location of the first disciples to be called *Christians* (Acts 11:25, 26).

Persecution Brought About Growth

Persecution is not considered to have a positive outcome on events; however, in this case it did because the Christians were compelled to leave Jerusalem and scatter, preaching the gospel wherever they stopped to rest and live. Luke described the results with these words: "Those who had been scattered preached the word wherever they went" (Acts 8:4).

Following his resurrection, Jesus explained to his disciples that once they received the Holy Spirit they were to become his witnesses, beginning in Jerusalem, then to Judea, next to Samaria and ultimately "to the ends of the earth" (Acts 1:8). Obviously, they were not moving quickly enough in carrying out his instruction, so the Lord gave them a nudge by allowing a great persecution to break "out against the church at Jerusalem" (Acts 8:1). The Christians had grown comfortable in Jerusalem and were reluctant to move into other areas. Their experience should serve as a warning to us, who have accepted the Gospel call to carry the good news to the ends of the earth.

Sometime later, Paul and Barnabas preached the good news at Derbe, Listra, Iconium and Antioch. The focus of their message was:

> We must go through many hardships to enter the *kingdom of God*. Paul and Barnabas appointed elders for them in each *church* and, with prayer and fasting, committed them to the Lord, in whom they had put their trust (Acts 14:22, 23, emphasis added).

Both *kingdom* and *church* appear in the same context in these two verses; therefore, we can only conclude that Paul and Barnabas were talking about the same thing. Continuing through chapter fifteen, there are six references to the church, and from this point forward, *the church*, generally, is the term used.

Summary

> It was the day of Pentecost when suddenly a violent wind, accompanied by tongues of fire, came down from heaven and rested upon the apostles. They began to communicate with the people in languages and dialects they had never learned.
>
> Peter stood up and explained that they were witnessing the fulfillment of Joel's prophecy (Joel 2:28-32).

The audience was overwhelmed with the apostle's remarks and asked what they should do. When given the answer, some 3000 were baptized for the forgiveness of their sins.

With this, a new movement began. It was first known as the kingdom, but later was called the church. The rapid growth led to Jealousy among the Pharisees, so they arrested Peter and John and had them put in jail over night.

A great persecution broke out against the church in Jerusalem that caused the disciples to leave the city, spreading the word about Jesus wherever they went, which resulted in churches springing up in numerous towns. One place where the church grew quickly was in Antioch of Syria.

Barnabas was one of the disciples who began working in Antioch. He traveled to the city of Tarsus and invited Saul (later to be known as Paul) to join him in the work in Antioch. The converts were first called Christians in Antioch.

Luke's remarks began with "Barnabas and Paul," in that order, but were soon reversed with Paul's name appearing first. No question exists about who was better qualified, but without Barnabas, the encourager, we may never have heard of Paul. People appreciate and respond favorably to encouragement.

Chapter Nine examines the organization of the church along with the different expressions used to identify those who make up the church.

The Church Belongs to Jesus Christ

It is reasonable to conclude that any reference to the church that fails to identify with the one to whom it belongs, will raise a problem within the Christian community.

Jesus called it "my church" (Matthew 16:18). He is said to be the "head of the body, the church" (Colossians 1:18). In the Ephesian letter, the apostle Paul wrote that "Christ is the head of the church, his body, of which he is the Savior" (Ephesians 5:23). In v.25, he adds that "Christ loved the church and gave himself up for her."

Strange, isn't it, how the religious community has departed so far from the Lord's admonition to identify themselves with terms that in no way relate to Jesus Christ!

CHAPTER 9

Unity and the Church

Review. Here is a brief summary of the mission of Jesus to this point:

- o Jesus introduces the *kingdom* of heaven also labeled *kingdom* of God.
- o Jesus announces his intent to build his *church* with the assurance that nothing would be able to overcome it.
- o The *church* is established in Acts of the Apostles and is first mentioned by word, in chapter 5:11.
- o Both words—*kingdom* and *church*—are used by way of clarification in Acts of the Apostles.
- o In Acts 11:26, the disciples are referred to for the first time as *Christians*.

By the time Paul's ministry begins, the word *church* appears far more frequently. *Church* is mentioned one hundred-three times following Acts 8:1 throughout the remainder of the New Testament, while *kingdom* is used twenty-eight times.

Kingdom and Church. References to the *kingdom* were not forgotten after churches were established. The following extensive—but by no means exhaustive—list of Scriptures demonstrates how Luke and Paul continued to keep the *kingdom* concept as part of their teaching:

Acts 8:12 Philip "preached the good news about the kingdom of God and the name of Jesus Christ." As a result, both men and women were being baptized.

Acts 14:22 Paul and Barnabas preached the good news regarding Jesus in Lystra, Iconium and Antioch. Their comment to the audience was, "We must go through many hardships to enter the kingdom of God."

Acts 19:8 While in Ephesus, "Paul entered the synagogue and spoke boldly there for three months, arguing persuasively about the kingdom of God."

Acts 20:25 To the Ephesian elders, Paul declared, "Now I know that none of you among whom I have gone about preaching the kingdom will ever see me again."

Acts 28:23 When Paul was taken to Rome as a prisoner, the Jewish brethren met with him to discuss what they had been hearing about his teaching and preaching. Luke records, "From morning till evening he explained and declared to them *the kingdom of God* and tried to convince them about Jesus from the Law of Moses and from the Prophets." These meetings continued for two years while Paul lived in rented quarters, and he taught all who visited him with these words: "Boldly and without hindrance he preached the *kingdom of God* and taught about the Lord Jesus Christ" (v. 30, emphasis added).

Romans 14:16, 17 "Do not allow what you consider good to be spoken of as evil. For the *kingdom of God* is not a matter of eating and drinking, but of righteous, peace and joy in the Holy Spirit,..." Paul uses the present tense, which means that the Roman Christians were experiencing "righteous, peace and joy in the Holy Spirit" in the kingdom at the time of his writing. The kingdom business is not eating and drinking—that is, physical and material behavior—but what relates to spiritual matters.

The *Church: Called out Christians*

The Greek word, *ekklesia,* with few exceptions, is translated "church" in the New Testament, but it was used by the Greeks long before the New Testament was written. The Greek world used the word to designate "the regular assembly of the whole body of citizens in a free-city state, 'called out' Greek 'out,'" (Gr *ek,* "out," and *kalein,* "to call") by the herald for the discussion and decision of public business."[1]

The translators of the Greek Septuagint version of Old Testament rendered the Hebrew word, *kahal,* in the Old Testament to denote "congregation" or "community" with reference to Israel. A similar use is found in the New Testament in Acts 7:38, employed by the disciple, Stephen, and generally translated in recent versions as "congregation" or "assembly." However, the KJV renders it as "church."

Also, a similar use of *kahal* in the Old Testament is rendered *ekklesia* in Acts 19:32, 38, 41 and translated into English as *assembly.* Paul's preaching in Ephesus had caused many Helenists to forsake their idolatrous practices and turn to Christ Jesus. Acts 19:20 states that the word of the Lord was growing mightily and prevailing. Demetrius, the silversmith, who made his living by selling idols fashioned as little gods, realized that Paul's teaching would destroy his business. He assembled men of similar trade and created a riot against Paul in the theater. As a result, the *ekklesia* (here translated "assembly" and not "church") was in confusion, and many did not know why they had come together (v. 32). Verses 38 and 41 also use the word "assembly". The town clerk was able to quiet the multitude and explained that if they had any further matter to resolve, they could take it up in the *ekklesia* (regular assembly, Acts 20:39). Since *ekklesia* means "to call out," in this instance people were called out of their homes, businesses, or fields into an assembly in the theater where they had gathered to be addressed by the town clerk. In other words, they had assembled together in one place. In a similar way, when the church (*ekklesia* or "called out ones") came together, they constituted an assembly.

Another example appears in 1 Corinthians 11 where Paul is instructing the Christians at Corinth regarding partaking of the Lord's Supper. He writes: "For first of all, when you come together (*en ekklesia,* translated "in the church") ... I hear that divisions exist among you; and I partly believe it" (v.18, ASV). They are "meeting together" and, as such, are an *ekklesia* or "assembly." So the church is a body of Christians, who has been called out of Satan's realm, the world, into the kingdom of Christ and God (Ephesians 5:5).

Colossians 1:13 comes closer to paralleling the meaning of the word "church" than any other passage in the New Testament. The New American Standard Version best translates the thought:

> For he delivered us from the domain of darkness, and transferred us to the kingdom of His beloved Son, in whom we have redemption, the forgiveness of sins (Colossians 1:13).

Paul is declaring that we have been called out of Satan's *realm,"domain* of darkness," and transferred or translated into the kingdom of Christ, "His beloved Son". This wording describes the church, *ekklesia,* with clarity.

Acts chapter two records the beginning point for the *kingdom,* designated the *church* in Acts 5:11. Luke described the miraculous events that took place on the day of Pentecost. The apostle Peter, as the primary spokesman, began his lesson by preaching Jesus and the resurrection. Near the end of chapter four, we read: "And with great power the apostles were giving witness to the resurrection of the Lord Jesus, and abundant grace was upon them all" (4:33, NASV).

Expressions Used to Identify the Called Out

1. *The Church,* Matthew 18:17

In Matthew 18, Jesus explained to his disciples how differences among them should be settled. First, the brother or sister should attempt to resolve the matter by personal contact. If this approach fails, one or two witnesses were to be brought into the discussion so that every fact can be confirmed. If there is still disagreement, the matter is to be taken before the church (v-17), indicating the entire congregation should be brought into the matter.

This approach is wise because it would encourage the wrongdoers to correct the matter. If no correction would be forthcoming the church as a body would need to be unified in applying church discipline. In this case, the church functions as a unit and stands together in whatever decision is reached.

A careful reading of the text, beginning with the book of Acts, reveals that the majority of the references to the church simply refer to it as "the church." By reading the context, the location of a specific congregation of the church usually can be determined. However, this point cannot always be decided since numerous references exist where the writer only intended to make a specific point—for example in I Corinthian 14:5, "so that the *church* may be edified." There are five other references to the church in this same chapter. In Philippians 3:6, Paul declared that he was "persecuting the church." In 4:15 he wrote: "not one church shared with me."

In 3rd John, the apostle has three similar references in verses 6, 9 and10. Verse 9 reads: "I wrote to the church." He gives no hint regarding where this congregation was located.

2. ***The Church in Jerusalem,*** **Acts 8:1**

Wherever a congregation of Christians meeting together was being discussed, they functioned as a unit and were governed by members within the group. They were not then—and are not now—expected to answer to any outside group. When leaders were appointed, they are referred to in the New Testament as elders and deacons. The terms overseers, shepherds and bishops are frequently used to describe the elders' responsibility. They were chosen from within the membership. No single elder or deacon presided, but always—and only—a plurality of men.

3. ***The Church of the Gentiles, Romans*** **16:4**

Early in the history of the church, a definite distinction was made between Jew and Gentile. In this context, the apostle Paul speaks collectively of a nationality, the Gentiles as opposed to the Jews. In the first chapter when the apostle was writing about the gospel, he declared: "I am not ashamed of the gospel, because it is the power of God for the salvation of everyone who believes, first for the Jew, then for the Gentile" (Romans 1:16).

4. ***The Churches of Asia,*** **1 Corinthians 16:19**

Again, the apostle writes in a collective sense, bringing together all the congregations throughout Asia. In this instance, he includes both Jew and Gentile.

5. ***All the Churches of Christ Send Greetings,*** **Romans 16:16**

By using this expression, Paul identifies the church in a universal way. The emphasis is placed on Christ Jesus, the Head of the church. The comment has been made that we cannot have the plural usage without the existence of the singular, which, of course, is true.

6. *Church of God,* 1 Corinthians 1:2; 10:32; 11:22; 15:19; 2 Corinthians 1:1

The apostle Paul's reason for using the expression "Church of God," in this context, is puzzling. It is understood that everything begins with God—a point that is covered extensively in 1 Corinthians 15:20-28, and will be examined carefully in describing what is to take place at the end of the Christian era in relation to the kingdom.

The apostle wanted to be certain that his readers got the message that God takes precedence over all of humanity. He is not only the Creator and Sustainer of the creation but, ultimately, will be the one who will consummate all things when time is no more.

In the same way, the apostle uses "Churches of Christ" he refers to "Churches of God," (1 Thessalonians 2:14; 2 Thessalonians 1:4). Paul refers to "God's household" (1 Timothy 3:15), which he states is "the church of the living God, the pillar and foundation of the truth." Hence, it is clear that "household" and "church" are used interchangeably.

God expects the church to teach and uphold the truth. We serve a *living* God, as Paul told the Athenian philosophers while standing on the Areopagus:

> The God who made the world and all things in it, since He is Lord of heaven and earth, does not dwell in temples made with hands; neither is He served by human hands, as though He needed anything, since He Himself gives to all life and breath and all things (Acts 17:24, 25, NASV).

7. *The Body of Christ,* Ephesians 4:12

In addressing the Christians at Ephesus, Paul explains how the Lord has arranged for some Christians to be apostles, some prophets, some evangelist and some pastors and teachers. The work of these people was to equip "the saints for the work of service, to the building up of *the body of Christ*" (Ephesians 4:11, 12, NASV, emphasis added). Here the "body" is used to identify the church. In this same context he declares, "There is *one* body." In 1Corinthians 12:20 the apostle writes: "But now there are many members, *but one body*" (NASV). The contrast is drawn between the physical body and the spiritual body, that is, the body of Christ. In each case there is only one body, but that body has many members.

In describing the human body, Paul mentions the foot, hand, ear, eye and hearing. He then makes a humorous point by commenting what a strange scene it would be if the whole body were nothing but a foot, a hand, or other body part. Indeed, it would be shocking to spot a hundred eighty pound eyeball rolling down the road! Do you suppose the apostle was expecting this thought to be misunderstood or perhaps abused, since he makes a point to repeat it more than once in 1 Corinthians, chapter twelve?

In the physical body, the feet serve one purpose, with hand, ear, and eye each serving their own designated purpose. So, too, in the spiritual body, the members possess different gifts, talents, and abilities. Some have the gift of speech, some of encouragement, some of teaching, some of service, and such like. All the members functioning together constitute a complete unit (read verses 28-31). This cooperation of different parts will keep the body healthy, eliminate division and assure growth.

Some people have interpreted the word, "member (s)," in 1 Corinthians 12;14, 18, 2O, 22 (NASV); translated (part (s), NIV), to mean differing religious groups. Since verse twenty-seven reads: "Now you are Christ's body and individually members of it" (NASV); there can be only one logical conclusion: the members are individual Christians. The remainder of chapter 12:28-31 proceeds to talk about apostles, prophets, teachers and other individuals possessing differing gifts. These are individual Christians, who collectively make up the spiritual body of Christ.

8. *House Churches,* Acts 18:1-3

Early in the history of Christianity, a member's home often served as the common meeting place where the church assembled. From the standpoint of convenience and cost, a member's home would have satisfied the requirement for a small group.

The New Testament does identify names of families where the church met in their home. In writing the letter to the Christians at Rome, Paul mentions Priscilla (or Prisca) and Aquila, a Jewish couple he had met at Corinth. Since they were tent makers, by trade, Paul stayed with them for a period of time (Acts 18:1-3). He refers in his greetings to Aquila and Prisca as "my fellow-workers in Christ Jesus" (Romans 16:3). In verse 5 he continues, "also greet the church that is in their house."

In writing the Corinthian letter, Paul mentions Aquila and Prisca along with "the church that meets at their house" (1 Corinthians 16:19). It is obvious that this couple was esteemed highly by the apostle for he states that, "who for my life risked their own necks" (Romans 16:4, NASV). He does not elaborate on the nature of this episode, but any matter important enough to save one's life would not be forgotten quickly.

In writing the Colossian letter, Paul greets the brethren in Laodicea as well as "Nympha and the church that is in her house" (Colossians 4:15). There is a variant reading in this verse that renders Nympha as male. In either case, the church assembled to worship in a family's home. Naturally, as congregations grew in numbers, they would have been forced to find larger meeting facilities.

9. *The Church of the Firstborn,* Hebrews 12:23

The writer of the book of Hebrews uses "the Church of the Firstborn" to contrast Moses ascending Mount Sinai to the New Covenant, which he identifies as Mount Zion. He elaborates by calling it (the church) "the heavenly Jerusalem, the city of the living God"

(12:22). He continues, "to the *church of the first born* whose names are written in heaven" (v.23, emphasis added). Although it is not obvious from this English translation, the word "firstborn" is plural in the Greek text, thus meaning "firstborn ones."

10. *The Way*

"The Way," as a term referring to the church appears three times in the Acts of the Apostles.

First appearance, Acts 9:2: Paul, who is still known as Saul, was seeking to wipe out the followers of Christ. Luke's way of expressing what Saul was doing reads:

> Now Saul, still breathing threats and murder against the disciples of the Lord, went to the high priest, and asked for letters from him to the synagogues at Damascus, so that if he found any belonging to *the Way*, both men and women, he might bring them bound to Jerusalem (9:1,2, NASV, emphasis added).

Since he refers to them as *disciples of the Lord*, we know he is referring to the followers of Jesus Christ. So "*the Way*" refers to Christians.

Second appearance, Acts 19: The Way is used while Paul is in Ephesus where he is "arguing persuasively about the kingdom of God" (v.8); however, some began to "publicly malign the Way" (v.9). Verse 23 indicates there was a "disturbance about the Way." In verse 8, the apostle is discussing the kingdom of God, whereas, in verse 9, Luke has him talking about the "*Way*," of which some were raising criticism. From these references, we can conclude that Paul could easily shift to comments about the kingdom while talking about the church. In the next "appearance of the Way," Paul refers to the time when "I persecuted this Way to the death, binding and putting both men and women into prisons" (Acts 22:4).

Third Appearance, Acts 24:14, 22: Paul appeared before Felix, the governor, where he declared that, "according to the Way which they call a sect, I do serve the God of our Fathers." The final reference in v. 22 indicates that Felix was quite familiar with people who were followers of the Way.

All of these passages, in some manner, refer to Paul's ministry. The conclusion to be drawn from these many citations is that it is proper to use any one of these terms to identify the Lord's spiritual family.

Jesus built the church, sacrificed his life for it, and is its Head and Savior; therefore, it is appropriate to call it the "Church of Christ" or "Christ's Church." It is equally scriptural to refer to it as "The Body of Christ." Since everything begins and will conclude with God, it is appropriate to use "Church of God." In other words, any expression used in the New Testament to identify the followers of Jesus is appropriate to use. To select one term and insist that it be used to the exclusion of the others obviously would be a mistake.

Identifying the church by a name that fails to honor the one who built it, or fails to give honor to the one who purchased it with his blood, or ignores the church's Head and Savior, will cause us to drift from a sure foundation. Nothing in the New Testament justifies or supports using names that glorify people.

Advantages of House Churches

Acts chapter 2 indicates that some three thousand persons responded to Peter's preaching on the day of Pentecost in Jerusalem and were baptized. What we do not know is how many of this number lived in Jerusalem and surrounding areas. No doubt there was such a large number that all of them could not have met to worship in one assembly. Most likely they began to meet in small groups in members' homes. A number of examples are mentioned in the New Testament about this type of gathering, which is a practice that solved the problem of having a special meeting place for the beginning of a new congregation. It would have been inexpensive and simple to cover the cost. The expense of travel would have been kept to a minimum, since all, or the majority of members, would have been able to walk to the facility. Keeping the group small would have encouraged every member to participate actively in the assembly. House churches made it easy to have close relationships and to know the needs and concerns of each member.

It is appropriate to note that referring to the meeting place as "house church" is not correct. Each example mentioned in the New Testament refers to a group that met in a member's home. Therefore, to be completely accurate, "house church" is a term that should be dropped.

Disadvantages of House Church

Naturally, meeting in a small group would create some disadvantages. In a large group, there would be more people with special talents and training to assume leadership positions. It is easier to create enthusiasm in larger groups. More funds would be available to do evangelistic outreach in a large church. Following the organization used in most churches today, a small group would not be able to pay a located preacher. It might also be difficult to have sufficient male members qualified to serve as elders and deacons.

One point that needs clarification is the manner in which people often refer to the church. Frequently, the *building* is referred to as *the church*. In a similar way, the expression "going to church" is commonly used. Of course, neither thought is Scriptural. The building is a convenient place for Christians (the church) to come together as a body to worship. In addition, we don't "go to church": We Christians are the church, even when not assembled.

The Religious World's Response

In light of Jesus' comment to Peter that "upon this rock I will build my church," (Matthew16:18, emphasis added), it is truly remarkable to observe the response of the religious world over the centuries.

Now, it is a given that the church is people and not a building. So when the church is mentioned, remember we are talking about the Lord's spiritual family—not a building. When Jesus declared, "I will build my church"—once accomplished—there is no reason for mistaking to whom the church belongs. He is the builder. Scripture teaches that he paid the required price for the church: "Be shepherds of the church of God, which he bought with his own blood" (Acts 20:28). The New American Standard Version translates the word for "bought" as "purchased with his own blood." Since Jesus built the church and paid the purchase price, he naturally holds the title to it. It belongs to him and not to anyone else.

What Happened?

One can get into an automobile and drive around any small town and locate dozens of church buildings. How many will have a sign out front or on the building with words that honor Jesus Christ in any way? Why? If the church belongs to Christ and he is the Head, why not identify where the worshipers meet with a sign that honors the Head? Can we not simply refer to ourselves as Christians?

How different the world would be if every religious group who proposes to follow Jesus Christ wore the same name, taught, believed and upheld the same message! If in addition, they worshiped only at the altar of the One who declared, "I am the way and the truth and the life. No one comes to the Father except through me" (John 14:6). One might say, "That's impossible!" Then I ask: "Who is to blame?" Did the Lord give us an imperfect system or has it been corrupted by our carelessness, pride, arrogance, disobedience, and such like? A reading of Romans 1:18-32, might be helpful at this time. Are we prepared to suggest that the Lord's system is too simple and must be tweaked to satisfy our curiosity and appeal to our sophistication? Or, does it really matter what we think?

Jesus—who was about to sacrifice his life on a Roman cross—urgently prayed for unity:

> Holy Father, protect them by the power of your name—the name you gave me—so that they may be one as we are one...I in them and you in me. May they be brought to *complete unity* to let the world know that you sent me and have loved them even as you have loved me (John 17:11, 23, emphasis added).

"Unity" continued to be a major theme in the Lord's prayer. He was concerned about unity among his disciples—the "them" of the following statement—but also our "unity" today.

> Sanctify them by the truth; your word is truth.... My prayer is not for them alone (the twelve apostles). I pray also for those who will believe in me through their message, that all of them may be one, Father, just as you are in me and I am in you (vv. 17, 20).

Unfortunately, we have ignored the Lord's earnest prayer for unity, harmony and oneness. How can we—today—engage in the search for unity that our Lord desired among his followers? Is it a lack of trust or, perhaps, determination to do things one's own way?

The need for unity also was a problem in the New Testament church. Paul wrestled with it in a small body of believers at Corinth while the church was still in its infancy:

- They were quarreling, bragging and dividing their allegiance.
- They were boasting about who had baptized them.

- Some proposed to identify with Paul, some with Apollos, some with Cephas and others with Christ.

Paul attempted to solve this sad situation by appealing to the Corinthian Christians in the name of the Lord Jesus Christ that they all agree with one another and be perfectly united in mind and thought (1 Corinthians 1:10 and following). A serious lesson can be learned from events in Corinth. Either we stand together, or if not, we are certain to fail. The expression, "United we stand—divided we fall" is a truism that Paul understood. As a result, he declared emphatically:

For I resolved to know nothing while I was with you except Jesus Christ and him crucified....My message and my preaching were not with wise and persuasive words, but with a demonstration of the Spirit's power, so that your faith might not rest on men's wisdom, but on God's power (1 Corinthians 2: 2, 4, 5).

The Meeting in Jerusalem

In Acts, chapter 15, Luke described how the New Testament church solved a major problem that was causing division. Church leaders gathered at Jerusalem to resolve the problem of circumcision that had arisen when Paul and Barnabas were establishing churches in Asia Minor. Brethren from Judea began to teach that circumcision and observance of the Law of Moses was necessary to be saved. The church commissioned Paul and Barnabas to travel to Jerusalem and place this matter before the apostles, elders and the whole church (Acts 15:1-4).

After much discussion, a consensus of views was reached and a letter was drafted and sent to the churches involved. Three significant points were covered in this discussion.

1. There were apostles present who could address the subject with the approval of the Holy Spirit.

2. The elders and the whole church were involved in the decision.
3. Very little of the New Testament had been written by now, so it was necessary for the apostles to be brought into the discussion, as they were specially gifted by the Holy Spirit.

Once the letter was read before the church, the whole body was satisfied with the answer to their concerns, and peace prevailed. The resolution of the problem involved the whole church, not the decision of one person. One important lesson learned from this was—disagreements and differences need to be addressed and settled quickly before they have time to spread and cause division. A discerning and thoughtful leadership will take action to put out the fires of discord before they spread.

On occasions, people who cause problems—such as, Jannes, Jambres and Diotrephes (2 Timothy 3:8; 3rd John v.9)—needed to be disciplined to avoid dissension within the church family. Fortunately, the Scriptures provide us with adequate instructions on how to handle such matters. Avoiding divisions requires the action of godly leaders whose goal is the salvation of every person.

Appointment of Leaders

Luke records that in the *church* at Antioch there were prophets and teachers, including Barnabas and Saul. It is interesting to note that, "While they were worshiping the Lord and fasting, the Holy Spirit said, 'Set apart for me Barnabas and Saul for the work to which I have called them'" (Acts 13:2). The frequency with which the Holy Spirit is mentioned in the ministry of the church leaders raises the question as to why so little attention is given to the operation of the Holy Spirit in today's church.

As Paul and Barnabas traveled throughout the Mediterranean world proclaiming the good news of Jesus, churches were established in major cities. By the time they returned for a visit, the churches had grown sufficiently, so they appointed elders in each church. They followed the appointment with prayer and fasting, which was their way of committing them to the Lord. The brief period of time that expired between the beginning of the congregation and the appointment of elders (also called "shepherds") was noticeably different when compared to how much time churches today take before selecting men to lead. Failure to train, select and appoint qualified leaders could result in a local congregation failing to grow and possibly end up being faced with unnecessary problems.

Why the Switch from Kingdom to Church?

No clear statement exists as to why the change was made from kingdom to church, but one can surmise that it was done for the sake of clarity. Perhaps it is because the church takes on a more personal nature. That certainly is true when the apostle introduced and developed the family and body concept.

In Ephesians 5, Paul begins to compare the husband-wife relationship to that of Christ and the church. He presents the husband as head of the wife just as Christ is the Head of the church. It follows that the church is subject to Christ in the same way that the wife is to be subject to her husband. Their relationship is to be sealed with love assuring its unity and harmony. This analogy helps us to appreciate the importance of our relationship with Christ because he sacrificed his life for the church, that is, for us who are Christians.

Body Illustration Easy to Understand

It was left to the apostle Paul to develop the concept of the church as the *body* of Christ. The *body* concept encourages the Christian to grasp the personal and intimate relationship of the kingdom and church. In his letter to the Corinthian Christians, Paul begins with the human body and explains how it consists of many members, which have different functions, serve different purposes and fulfill different roles. For example, the eyes provide vision; the ears, hearing; the hands, feeling and movement; the feet, walking and running. In a healthy body every member carries out his or her role or function; therefore, by working together the body is able to accomplish every good purpose necessary for life (1 Corinthians 12).

Paul then explains how the Lord's spiritual body consists of many members—just as many as there are individual Christians. Not all members serve the same purpose or fill identical roles. Some are evangelists, some pastors, some teachers, some helpers, some administrators, but all serving together constitute the *one body of Christ* (1 Corinthian 12:12-31). His point is that each member carries out his or her role or function so that, while working together, the body is able to function in accordance with its intended purpose.

By working in a harmonious way, every need is supplied. No member is neglected since the members have the same care for each other. If one member suffers, all suffer together; if one member is honored, all rejoice together (12:26). The thought is completed with the following: "Now you are the body of Christ and individually members of it" (v 27, RSV).

Using this analogy of the church:

- Christ becomes the Head (Ephesians 5:23; Colossians 1:18, 24).
- Christians are the subjects or members (Acts 11:26).
- The New Covenant is the Law by which they are governed.
- The world constitutes the territory where all the members serve.

Comparing this analogy with the kingdom, the one unique difference is that Christ is the King, whereas here, he becomes the Head of the Body.

- In the Ephesian context, Jesus Christ, in addition to being the Head, is also the Savior of the body (Ephesians 5:23).
- In the Colossian context, Paul specifies that the body is the church.

Therefore, the church and the body are one and the same and have one Head, Jesus Christ. The church is subject to its head, Jesus Christ, and no other (Ephesians 5:24). Peter stated that "there is salvation in no one else" (Acts 4:12).

What matters is that all the members are performing their assigned task cooperatively so as to keep the body healthy while accomplishing the purpose for which each one exists. A healthy body is recognized where every member is performing according to his or her intended purpose. The family and body concepts focus on relationship because every member counts. No member is unimportant, and when working together in a harmonious way, good things are accomplished.

Paul's comparison of the physical body with the spiritual body simplifies our understanding of Christ's spiritual body. It is clear that there is only *one* body. It is also true that this one body possesses only one Head, Jesus Christ. It's equally true that the one body consists of many members, just as many as there are individual Christians. It also follows that the members need to function in a harmonious manner for unity and peace to prevail. These members need to possess a genuine concern for each other, since they are dependent on one another for body growth and vitality. In considering the harmony essential for a compatible spiritual relationship, the apostle Paul includes the following in Ephesians 5:21, "Submit to one another out of reverence to Christ."

It is much like an automobile engine; the car performs best when the engine is hitting on all cylinders. In much the same way, the church as the body of Christ performs best when every member is contributing his or her assigned function or gift.

In our family-body relationship, we are dealing with principles that can be transposed readily into the spiritual dimension. Paul's use of the word "household" immediately comes to mind in making the transition from the physical to the spiritual realm. The Holy Spirit chose the correct analogy when he had the apostles introduce the family-body concept to simplify and enhance our understanding of the Kingdom and the Church.

Unique References to the Church

References to the *church* occur with considerable frequency in the New Testament because it is such an important subject. The following is a listing of a few references with a brief description of their context.

- Acts 5:11 "Great fear seized the whole *church*" following the death of Ananias and Sapphira.
- Acts 8:1 "On that day a great persecution broke out against the *church* at Jerusalem."
- Acts 8:3 "Saul began to destroy the *church*."
- Acts 11:22 "News...reached the ears of the *church* at Jerusalem."
- Acts 11:26 "So for a whole year Barnabas and Saul met with the *church* and taught great numbers of people."
- Acts 12:1 "King Herod arrested some who belonged to the *church* intending to persecute them."
- Acts 12:5 "The *church* was earnestly praying to God" for Peter.
- Acts 14:23 "Paul and Barnabas appointed elders for them in each *church*."
- Acts 14:27 Paul and Barnabas "gathered the *church* together and reported all that God had done."

There are five additional references in Acts, chapter fifteen. From this list, it is obvious that every event that took place involves the *church*. Seldom is the word *kingdom* used to identify the movement or to describe what was taking place.

Summary

Both terms—*kingdom* and *church*—are used in the Book of Acts to identify Christians. Beginning with Paul's ministry, the *church* appears with greater frequency.

The Greek world first used "ekklesia" to identify a regular assembly of people. It was first used in Christianity by Jesus in Matthew 16:18 as the "called out ones" and translated in English as *church*.

Expressions used to identify these people are "The Church; Churches of Christ; Church of God; Body of Christ; Church of the Firstborn; The Way; the church in a specific location, ie., The Church in Jerusalem; The Churches of Asia.

In early history, small groups met in homes.

The religious world's way of identifying the *church* frequently uses titles associated with an individual's name or title.

The problem of division was solved by the group who met in Jerusalem.

Paul and Barnabas appointed elders in churches they had established.

> Paul used body language to identify the church as the *Body of Christ.*

Chapter 10 covers a brief summary of the *Purpose of the Church.* The importance of what one believes and where to find the correct answers is included.

The Church Satisfies All of Our Needs

God designed us so that it is essential for us to be together in order to reproduce and continue to live upon the earth. In the very beginning, "The Lord God said: 'It is not good for the man to be alone. I will make him a helper suitable for him" (Genesis 2:18).

God knows we need companionship, togetherness, and fellowship. That's why He made Eve to serve as a companion for Adam. It also explains why Jesus said: "Upon this rock I will build my church, and the gates of Hades will not overcome it" (Matthew 16:18).

Jesus knows we do not function well as individuals. We need fellowship and companionship. The church satisfies that need in a remarkable way. God through Jesus supplies our every need.

"What is impossible with men is possible with God" (Luke 18:27).

CHAPTER 10

The Purpose of the Church

When God created the human race, He designed us with a need for companionship, association, togetherness and fellowship. Therefore, Jesus prepared the church as a spiritual body in order to satisfy our need for close relationships and fellowship. Coming together on the Lord's Day or First Day of the Week to honor and praise him through our collective worship not only serves to fulfill our need for fellowship, but it meets our need to assemble together (Hebrews 10:25).

Not only are we edified (which means "built up") in our love for the Lord, who so willingly left heaven and came to this sinful world to save and deliver us from Satan and sin, but we are filled with joy and radiance that words cannot express adequately. In addition, church assemblies draws and binds us together with *cords* that cannot be broken easily. Circumstances in life can become such that we need reaffirmation regarding our core beliefs, and the encouragement received from others helps us through difficult times.

The Lord views us as being special. Peter describes it with admirable beauty:

> But you are a chosen people, a royal priesthood, a people belonging to God, that you may declare the praises of him who called you out of darkness into his wonderful light. Once you were not a people, but

> now you are the people of God; once you had not received mercy, but now you have received mercy (1Peter 2:9,10).

The following descriptions of the content of church assemblies every first day of the week (Sunday) help us to see the wonderful blessings that come from assembling with other believers:

- *Studying God's Word*. The spiritual strength and comfort received from reading and listening to the Scriptures reaffirms our confidence and increases our faith in the Lord. The writer of the book of Hebrews uses impressive language to describe the word: "For the word of God is living and active. Sharper than any double-edge sword" (4:12). It activates the mind and can filter out the trash and rubbish to where our thoughts are pure and our actions obtain the approval of our Creator. There is great joy, satisfaction and contentment derived from reading and meditating on the Scriptures. The apostle calls it, *the word of truth, the gospel of our salvation,* that *gives us hope,*—all "to the praise of his glory" (Ephesians 1:12-14).
- *Singing.* Blending our voices in melodious songs inspires and touches our hearts; moreover, the desire to please our Lord grows exponentially. Nothing moves the emotions more than making melody with the human voice as together we harmonize the words of great spiritual songs and hymns. (Ephesians 5: 17-20; 1Corinthians 16:2).
- *The Lord's Supper.* Participating in the Lord's Supper each first day of the week moves us emotionally to where it is difficult to hold back the tears. We pick up the unleavened bread and call to mind the broken body of our Savior, who willingly was whipped, scourged and beaten until he was unable to carry the burden of his cross. Then we take the fruit of the vine and, by faith, we remember the blood of our Redeemer flowing freely from his pummeled body. We press

the cup to our lips realizing that it represents the life of One who was innocent but willingly offered himself as a sacrifice for the guilty. This service tugs at our heartstrings and draws us into a closer and deeper relationship with Jesus, who loves us so much, and loved the people nailing him to a cross in a cruel death. Looking at those men who hammered nails into his hands and feet, his love was shown in some of his dying words: "Father, forgive them, for they do not know what they are doing" (Luke 23:34).

➢ *Contributions.* Our monetary giving, generally done during our public assembly on the first day of the week, should not be overlooked. The Scripture tells us that, "God loves a cheerful giver" (2 Corinthians 9:8). Jesus declared that a generous giver will be rewarded: "Give and it will be given to you; good measure, pressed down, shaken together, running over, they will pour into you lap" (Luke 6:38). The master has promised to reward generous, cheerful givers. In my more than 90 years, I have yet to hear anyone disagree or deny that this principle is true.

We can give in many ways other than of our material or monetary resources; for example, we can give of our time to assist and comfort others, whatever the need. We can share the Gospel with people who are searching for truth and want to know what they must do to be saved. As his ambassador in this world, you can think of other good ways to serve and give to others in the name of Jesus Christ. We obtain great satisfaction and comfort from giving of ourselves. In 2 Corinthians 5:20, Paul writes: "We are therefore Christ's ambassadors, as though God were making his appeal through us. we implore you on Christ's behalf: Be reconciled to God."

➢ *Invitation to obey the gospel.* The Scriptures teach in many ways that the primary objective of the church is the salvation of souls. Luke penned the following words to impress us with what Jesus came to do: "For the Son of man has come to seek

> and to save that which was lost" (Luke 19:10). Each of us can help in this effort. Our gift may not be teaching, but we can assist the person who is a gifted teacher. We may be able to provide a desirable meeting place for lessons to be taught. If there are children that need to be entertained or cared for while adults are being taught, that may be where someone can serve. Providing transportation, if needed, is another way to be involved.

Sometimes evangelists, preachers, teachers leave the impression that every Christian must be actively involved in leading a non-Christian to Christ. Is it required that every Christian must convert someone? I answer, "No." Christians have different gifts, talents and abilities, which is the point of Paul's teaching regarding the body in 1 Corinthians, chapter 12. What matters is that members use the gifts with which God has blessed us to accomplish His purpose. Together, we are to use our gifts for the common good.

To sum up the purpose of the church: it is a sweet fellowship (or *koinonia* to use the Greek word) shared by Christians, which surpasses all other relationships. The closest thing to it is the physical family, more specifically, the husband and wife relationship where there is a genuine bond. However, marriage does not bind husband and wife together in the same way as does our relationship with our God through Jesus Christ. The reason is obvious: in our wonderful spiritual relationship, we are participating in eternal benefits—life beyond the grave. Praise God!

The Husband-wife Relationship Compared to Christ and the Church

Paul used the analogy of the husband and wife in marriage to portray the relationship of Christ and the church: "the husband is the head of the wife, as Christ also is the head of the church, He Himself being the Savior of the body" (Ephesians 5:23, NASV). He follows this thought with the statement that the church is subject to Christ as the wife is to be to her husband (v.24).

The next point is where many husbands fail the test: "The husband is to love his wife just as Christ loved the church and gave himself up for her" (v.25). Christ sacrificed his life for the church. When a devoted and loving husband is ready to sacrifice himself for his wife, one would have difficulty prying a Christian bride away from him. Unfortunately, in our culture today, few husbands fit this mold.

A perfectly committed relationship is exactly what was portrayed by Christ who loved the church and gave himself up for her. In so doing, he sanctified and cleansed the church by the washing of water with the word. He further presented the church to himself in all her glory without spot or wrinkle, but that she should be holy and blameless (Ephesians 5:22-30). Such a family relationship, whether physical or spiritual, would be a great help in preparing for eternal life.

Does It Matter What One Believes?

Many times, while involved in religious conversations with others, the comment is made that it does not matter what you believe as long as you are sincere. It goes without saying that *insincerity* will disqualify us. But let's examine a few Scriptures and decide if the comment—"it does not matter what you believe as long as you are sincere"—is valid. Note the words of Jesus:

> Not every one who says to me, Lord, Lord, will enter the kingdom of heaven; but he who does the will of My Father who is in heaven. Many will say to Me on that day, Lord, Lord, did we not prophesy in Your name, and in Your name cast out demons, and in Your name perform many miracles?' And then I will declare to them, 'I never knew you; depart from Me,

> you who practice lawlessness' (Matthew 7:21-23, NASV).

Luke records Jesus admonishing his disciples with the following thought: "And why do you call Me, 'Lord, Lord,' and do not do what I say?" (Luke 6:46, NASV). Both Matthew and Luke give very strong words of admonition in these passages. Calling Jesus "Lord" will save no one who is not earnestly seeking to do the will of the Father. Whatever we may be doing or performing in His name accomplishes nothing relating to our eternal needs unless we are doing what He commands. When individuals practice lawlessness, their behavior is contrary to the law of Christ (Galatians 6:2).

John, in his gospel, records an account of Jesus being involved in conversation with a group of Pharisees who challenged his testimony. To those who were claiming to be children of Abraham, he declared: "If you hold to my teaching, you are really my disciples. Then you will know the truth, and the truth will set you free" (John 8: 31:32). The teaching of Jesus is recorded in the New Testament. Following his teaching will assure that we really are his disciples who are living by the truth. His truth is what will set us free from Satan and sin.

The writers of the New Testament are careful to spell out in no uncertain terms what manner of person each of us is to be in order to receive the Lord's blessing and to obtain his approval. The message is not difficult to understand, but does require an open mind and an honest heart. The ultimate requirement is our desire and willingness to trust and obey what is taught in the word.

Other expressions frequently heard in religious conversations are: "Join the church of your choice" or "One church is good as another." These comments ring somewhat hollow when one begins to examine the Scriptures. There is nothing taught in the Bible or God's word that indicates we are given a choice. Please review the following Scriptures regarding the church made by Jesus Christ and his apostles.

1) Jesus promised to build the church and he called it "My church" Matthew 16:18
2) The church is referred to as "the Body of Christ" (Colossians 1:24).
3) Jesus is declared to be "the Head of the Body" (Colossians 1:18).
4) Jesus is the "Savior of the Body" (Ephesians 5:23).
5) Jesus purchased the church with his blood (Acts 20:28).
6) It is called "the church of God" (1 Corinthians 1:2), since God is "over all and through all and in all" (Ephesians 4:6).

In light of these Scriptures, it seems reasonable for a church to wear a name that honors the God who created us, and Jesus Christ who redeemed us. To do otherwise is disrespectful toward its builder, head and savior, who purchased the church with his blood.

Why So Many Different Churches?

The church belongs to Christ by virtue of the fact that he built it, paid the purchase price and is its Head and Savior. Question: What has happened in today's religious world that has resulted in a multiplicity of churches wearing different names and teaching different doctrines yet are expecting to be saved by the same Lord?

Human nature being what it is, we don't always see things alike, nor do we always interpret information that we read in the same way. The comment is often heard that two things exist regarding which people seldom agree and can be very adamant about—religion and politics. The fact that religion affects almost every phase of our life on earth, and what happens after we die, it is no surprise that we devote so much time to what it means to us. If we are serious, and it seems reasonable to assume that most people are, then we obviously are concerned that we *get it right*. This fact often leads to disagreements that divide churches. Then what can we do? Generally, we go our separate ways and frequently end up starting a new group that is given a different name. Usually, we feel compelled to come up with different teaching that separates us from the original group. By last count more than 350 denominations were identified in the United States, and the number is growing.

Sometimes a strong-willed person insists on leading and demanding his/her own way about things. If this individual is questioned or challenged regarding a position held, it usually is just a matter of time until such a one is ready to break away and start another group that he or she can control. The result: another *church*. In my sixty-five years of preaching I have personally seen this happen numerous times.

Others have broken away and started what they refer to as "High Church," which is a way of identifying a sophisticated group who think of themselves as being better educated and a cut above others. It is only natural that they are going to introduce forms of worship that set them apart from others from whom they have pulled away. A new name is chosen and the list continues to grow.

Questions are raised from the consequences of Christians losing sight of two important spiritual concepts: (a) To whom does the church belong? and (b) Who is the head of the church? Answer: People become careless and begin to drift away from the anchor point. This spiritual drift happened within the Corinthian church after Paul had finished his work there and moved to another location. The people there were missing a strong leader and were not blessed with written instruction as we are today. At that time, very little of the New Testament had been written and what was recorded was not available in sufficient quantities to be widely circulated among the churches. This situation left the door open to teachers inclined to branch out and propose their own new ideas.

Consequently, it comes as little surprise to hear some Corinthians saying "we are prepared to go along with what Paul proposed;" others; "we like what Apollos presented;" still others, "Cephas (or Peter's) approach makes better sense to us." Last of all, a few others were saying: "We want to be sure we are doing what Christ approves." The result was a group of worshipers with little in common who were not enjoying close fellowship and unity.

Where Does This Leave One Searching for Truth?

We live in a world populated by Christians, atheists, agnostics, infidels, unbelievers and a multitude of religious people practicing a variety of religious faiths. So, what shall the innocent party do—who for the first time in life takes an interest in religion? One is indeed fortunate who is born into a religious environment where the Bible is found, where God is honored, and where Jesus Christ is worshiped as the Son of God. Even then, such a person faces critical decisions regarding where to worship, since there exists a multitude of different churches.

The answer to the question raised in the previous paragraph—when given the opportunity to help an honest, sincere person searching for truth,—is to follow the admonition of the apostle Paul who exhorted the Ephesian Christians to "speak the truth in love" (Ephesians 4:15). I am reminded of the line in Julie Andrews song: "A spoon full of sugar makes the medicine go down in a most delightful way." Indeed it does! It is true that we catch more flies with honey than we do with vinegar.

Why is Christianity Constantly Criticized?

Christianity has received more criticism than all the other religions of the world combined. Why? Because Christianity is founded on the Bible which is God's word. The Bible begins by introducing God, the Creator of the heavens and the earth (Genesis 1:1). Creation, in its entirety, is attributed to God, who in the Hebrew text is called *Elohim*.

According to the Bible, the whole of creation was completed in six days, and God rested on the seventh day.

The Bible states that God is Spirit (John 4:24), and as such He is eternal, without beginning or conclusion. In other words, He has always existed! He existed before this world began and will continue to exist when this world is no more. He is a perfect, eternal being, never having made a mistake, or, committed a sin and always does what is right. He is worthy!

Only one other personality can claim perfection as does this God of the Bible, and that is the Lord Jesus Christ. John, the writer of the fourth Gospel, identifies Jesus as the Word (*Logos*): "In the beginning was the Word, and the Word was with God, and the Word was God. He was in the beginning with God" (John 1: 1, 2). John attributes the creation to the *Logos*—"And the Word became flesh and dwelt among us"—referring to Jesus Christ (v. 14).

These two eternal, all-powerful, supernatural beings separate Christianity from every other religion. Christianity lays claim to a living Savior who was crucified, nailed to a cross, placed in a borrowed tomb and on the third day rose to live again forever (Matthew 27:33-66; 28:1-20). No other religion in today's world can make a similar claim. Moreover, this same Jesus claims to be the Savior of the world:

> "For the Son of Man came to seek and to save that which was lost" (Luke19:10).
>
> "I am the way, and the truth, and the life; no one comes to the Father, but through Me" (John14:6).

We can refuse to accept Jesus' claim stated in these verses, but Paul writes that, at a specific time, we will come face to face with it:

> Every knee will bow and every tongue will confess that Jesus Christ is Lord to the glory of God the Father (Philippians 2:9-11).

Everyone, eventually, will be faced with the evidence of a risen Savior, the Lord Jesus Christ when he returns.

The Bible, A Unique Volume

The Bible, without question, is the most unique and amazing book in the world! It is unique because of a single plan and purpose woven throughout its pages. It tells us from where we came, why we are here and where we are going when life ends here.

The Bible consists of sixty-six books, thirty-nine in the Old Testament and twenty-seven in the New Testament. It was written by kings, peasants, fishermen, shepherds and educated people—some 40 in number over a period of 1500 years. It was written on three continents—Asia, Africa, and Europe—in three languages—Hebrew, Aramaic and Greek. It deals with hundreds of controversial subjects, yet there is a continuity about it that defies human imagination. While its pages were being recorded, scientific discoveries were being made and learning changed the course of thought; however, nothing in the Bible is out of harmony with the known facts of science or any other truth in possession of the human race. This conclusion is to be expected, because the Bible states that "men moved by the Holy Spirit spoke from God" (2 Peter 1:20, 21). Paul wrote to the young convert Timothy:

"All Scripture is inspired by God and profitable for teaching, for reproof, for correction, for training in righteousness; that the man of God may be adequate, equipped for every good work" (2 Timothy 3:16, 17, NASV).

It is important to note that the word "man" in this passage is used without reference to gender.

Much more could be said about the Bible, but we conclude with a brief comment on the fruit borne by the Bible over the centuries. Wherever its teachings and influences have gone, nations and people have moved toward moral, physical, intellectual and spiritual development and progress—a fact that cannot be disputed.

No better example of the Bible's fruit exists than the United States of America. The people responsible for laying the nation's foundation built it around principles drawn from the Bible. Unfortunately, there are efforts being pushed in our national, state and local governments along with our colleges, universities and local educational systems to remove God and the Bible from the agenda.

Summary

Our Heavenly Father knows we need close relationships and fellowship to remain spiritually strong.

Church assemblies on the first day of each week provide time to: study God's word; sing melodious songs that inspire and touch our hearts; participate in the Lord's Supper; give of our monetary possessions to assist those in need, and share in sweet fellowship that helps to keep us spiritually healthy.

It is important to believe and follow what the Lord approves.

Several reasons are given explaining why there are so many different churches.

Christianity is criticized constantly because it claims to be inspired by God.

Numerous reasons are given as to why the Bible claims to be the word of God.

> Wherever the teachings and influence of the Bible have gone, nations and peoples moral, intellectual, spiritual and physical development have advanced in every respect.

The next chapter makes an appeal for *unity among the people of God* and emphasizes the only means by which it will ever happen—loving one another as Jesus Christ loves us.

Section Three

That We all Might be One

Jesus Knew Unity Would Be the Key to Church Growth.

His longest prayer is to the Father in John 17 where he makes an earnest appeal on behalf of the disciples that they would be united as "one" in the same manner he and the Father are "one."

It's no surprise to find that the greatest hindrance to church growth is division within the body. By the middle of the first century, people at Corinth were using a plurality of names to identify their following. Despite the effort of men like Paul, the apostle, to correct this matter, others have seen little reason to be guided by Jesus' comment: "Sanctify them by the truth; your word is truth" (John 17:17). Today, there is a multiplicity of churches wearing different names with little in common.

"It is true that some preach Christ out of envy and rivalry, but others out of good- will.... But what does it matter? The important thing is that in every way, whether from false motives or true, Christ is preached. And because of this I rejoice." Philippians 1:15-18).

CHAPTER 11

Resolving Disagreements

Introduction: Jesus and unity. Jesus knew that disagreements would arise even among the chosen twelve apostles. The entire seventeenth chapter of John's Gospel is devoted to Jesus' intercessory prayer where he appeals to the Father for the disciples to be united. Verse 11 begins, "that they may be one as we are one." It is somewhat remarkable to observe the number of times the previous thought is repeated throughout the chapter. In verses 21—23 he admonishes them to be one, "just as you are in me and I am in you.... May they be brought to complete unity to let the world know that you sent me and have loved them even as you have loved me." Earlier in v.17 his appeal was that the Father would, "Sanctify them by the truth; your word is truth." The word of truth was given to these men to guide and encourage them to remain true to the Lord.

Following this strong admonition by the Lord for unity to exist within the body, it comes as no surprise to find the apostle Paul devoting considerable time and effort to this subject.

Three examples of handling church disagreements. Paul discussed three examples of disagreements in the church that serve as models for our achieving the goal of unity

First example: Church at Corinth divided

Identifying religious bodies with names that fail to honor Christ, who is the Head and Savior of the Body, causes division and makes unity impossible. The apostle Paul was confronted with this problem at Corinth. There were factions within the group, creating quarrels and disputes. Some were saying, "I follow Paul;" another, "I follow Apollos;" another, "I follow Cephas;" still another, "I follow Christ" (1 Corinthians 1:12). Can you just imagine how heated that discussion was getting? It seems that the debate among the Corinthian Christians was very intense. Most of us would be thankful that we have never been involved in this kind of heated argument.

Undoubtedly, the apostle asked for additional wisdom before giving his answer. It would have been easy for him to lose his cool and reply: "What in the name of heaven is going on?" Instead, he asked in a calm way, "Is Christ divided? Was Paul crucified for you? Were you baptized into the name of Paul?" (v.13).

A reading of the remainder of the chapter reveals that Paul kept the emphasis off of himself or anyone other than Jesus Christ. The real test of a true apostle shines forth in chapters two and three. You may want to read these chapters carefully and savor the beauty with which the apostle handled this very delicate problem.

Second example: New convert versus one mature in faith

In his letter to the Christians at Corinth, Paul, in chapter eight, addressed a disagreement that had arisen between mature and weak brethren. It dealt with eating meat that had been sacrificed in pagan temples as a form of idol worship.

This meat was later being sold in the meat market and Christians who were mature in the faith purchased the meat and ate it with a clear conscience. The problem arose with new converts, weak in their faith and understanding, whose conscience would not permit them to eat this meat. This was leading to division in the church because to the weak brother it was a *faith issue* and wrong.

By way of clarification, the apostle wrote:

> So then, about eating food sacrificed to idols: We know that an idol is nothing at all in the world and that there is no God but one...the Father, from whom all things came and for whom we live; and there is but one Lord, Jesus Christ, through whom all things came and through whom we live. But not everyone knows this (1 Corinthians 8:4-7).

He continues by saying that eating food does not bring us near to God; so we are no worse if we don't eat and no better if we do. (v. 8).

Similar examples appear in some churches today out of questions surrounding fellowship meals held in the church building. The apostle's admonition to the Christians at Corinth is to be careful how you exercise your freedom that you do "not become a stumbling block to the weak" (v.9). He goes farther to caution the mature Christian that, "if what I eat causes my brother to fall into sin, I will never eat meat again." (8:13).

This issue of eating meat sacrificed to idols along with the *observance of special days* is discussed at length in the next chapter under the title, *Maintaining Peace While Settling Differences*. You may want to examine it carefully because Paul does an outstanding job in Romans chapter fourteen of explaining how to resolve problems that appear in the church, as well as in daily living.

If every phase of our life were evaluated on the basis of righteousness, peace and joy in the Holy Spirit, (Romans 14:17) there would be fewer doctor visits, additional longevity tacked on to the end of life and few, if any, regrets when the time arrived to make our journey into the eternal realm.

Third example: controversy over circumcision

Questions raised in the two examples above led to controversy between the Jews and the Gentiles. The apostle Peter, while visiting the church at Antioch in Syria, severed his table fellowship with the Gentile Christians because of questions raised by the circumcision group among the Jews. Paul accused these Jews of being hypocritical and failing to act "in line with the truth of the gospel" (Galatians 2:14). The critical problem centered on *their justification* regarding which Paul declared:

we know that man is not justified by the works of the Law, but by the faith *of* Jesus Christ. Hence we also believe in Christ Jesus, that we may be justified by the faith *of* Christ, and not by the works of the Law; because by the works of the Law no man will be justified (Galatians 2:16, *Confraternity Version*, emphasis added).

This issue led to a strong disagreement between Peter and Paul, in which Paul reminded Peter that he was living like a Gentile while, in reality, a Jew. In so doing, he was expecting Gentiles to follow Jewish customs.

Since the change from emphasis on *the kingdom* to discussion about *the church* begins primarily with Paul's teaching and ministry, it is interesting to note how at times he reverts back to conversations about the kingdom. The previous reference is a perfect example. It seems reasonable to conclude that the apostle is not intending to make any clear distinction between *the kingdom* and *the church.*

Choice of New Name

The name of the church has been changed throughout history that constitutes a great obstacle to our search for unity among Christians today. The Lord established his church and the New Testament records the names assigned to it by inspiration of the Holy Spirit.

The object is to compare these names with the different names that follow in the next paragraph.

The names given to the Lord's church are:

> "The Church" (in whatever location), "ex. at Jerusalem" Acts 8:1).
> "Church of Christ" (Romans 16:16).
> "Church of God" (1Corinthians 1:2).
> "The Body of Christ" (1Corinthians 12:27).
> "The Church of the Firstborn" (Hebrews12:23).

Some new titles given to the churches established in the centuries following the establishment of the Lord's church on Pentecost in Acts 2 are based on names of the founder-often without the founder's permission—making them obstacles to the unity that Jesus prayed about. No united approach among Christians can result as long as hundreds of churches exist on a human foundation with man-substituted names and teachings not found in God's Word.

Suggestion to the reader: go to the "yellow pages" of your local telephone book and examine the names under the heading of "Churches." Looking in a directory from a city in North Carolina revealed names of local churches not listed in the Scriptures:

- Names of churches with no connection to Jesus—"Glory Tabernacle," "Community Movement," "Sycamore Temple," "New Beginnings Christian Fellowship," "Church of the Rock."
- Names of movements started by men: "Methodist," "New Hope Presbyterian church."
- Names associated with a national or ethnic group: "St. Nicholas Russian Orthodox Church," "Mennonite Church." (People from a different national or ethnic group would likely not feel welcome in such a church.)

- Names of good men who followed Jesus in his ministry, but are not worthy of having a church named after them: "St. Luke's Church," St. Timothy's Mission."

  Question: How can we be united in a society with almost 300 churches boasting names of men and groups not found in the New Testament? The obvious answer to this question is: WE CANNOT! Unity will come only when we return to the teachings of the Lord Jesus Christ who made the supreme sacrifice for the church and labeled it "my church" (Matthew 16:18), indicating the church belongs solely and entirely to Jesus Christ.

In recent years, there has been a tendency of many religious groups to change their church's name from that which they used since their beginning. A short distance from where I attend worship regularly, there is a church building that for many years had a sign out front that read "Assembly of God." That sign has been changed to read "Genesis Church." Perhaps the younger generation was turned off by the older name and was looking for change closer to expressions used in Scripture. In many instances, this type of appeal might attract a larger audience. What ultimately matters most is what the people are being taught once they start attending. Has this change created a greater effort to preach and teach truth? If so, one could pronounce it an improvement.

However, one would find difficulty concluding that this name change from "Assembly of God" to "Genesis Church" is more Biblical. It is true that the word "Genesis" means *"beginning,"* but it is never used in Scripture to identify the church.

This tendency has been making its way into our fellowship recently. Some leaders have concluded that people are prejudiced toward the "Church of Christ" and consequently will not visit or meet with us. There may be some validity to that statement, but the Scriptures admonish us to "speak the truth in love" (Ephesians 4:14-16). Any departure from teaching and preaching the *truth in love*—with the right attitude—risks bringing the Lord's anathema (curse) down upon us (1 Corinthians 16:22; 2 John vv. 9-11). We who are members of the Church of Christ must be on guard to present an accurate picture of the church in our preaching and teaching. For example, we should not speak of the "Church of Christ" as if this were the only name that accurately identifies the church because it is not true and leaves a false impression with students of the word. It will cause them to look upon us as belonging to nothing more than another denomination.

Perhaps we are partially to blame for having failed to present an accurate picture of the church in our preaching and teaching. The fact is that all of the expressions describing the church: "The Church" (in whatever location), "Church of Christ," "Church of God," "The Body of Christ," "The Church of the Firstborn" are all Scriptural terms. We can use one or all of them, but to choose one and isolate the rest leaves the wrong impression. It deserves repeating:

> To identify a body of believers with words that honor someone other than Jesus Christ or God the Father is to dishonor the One who laid down his life to atone for our sins.

The Church Organized

It was noted earlier that following Peter's sermon on the day of Pentecost (Acts 2), some three thousand people responded to the message and were baptized (Acts 2:41). This event began a movement that required developing an organization to go forward. It was only natural that the apostles would provide the direction since Jesus had selected them to be the leaders. As expected, Luke states that the people were devoting themselves to four important elements of the apostles leadership: teaching, fellowship, breaking of bread, and prayer (v-42).

These people began a daily routine of meeting together in the temple for instruction. Since many of them had come from considerable distance to celebrate the feast, they were not prepared to stay beyond that observance. This fact explains Luke's report that many of the local Christians were selling their property and possessions to share with the ones who had needs (v.45). Nothing is said regarding how long this continued. We do know that they were praising God and gaining the favor of all the people. The church continued to grow, since "the Lord was adding to their number day by day those who were being saved" (Acts 2:47).

The reference to "breaking of bread" in verse 42 generally is interpreted to refer to the Lord's Supper. Verse forty-six explains that they were taking their meals together. Thus, "breaking bread" in this verse is questionable as to its meaning.

This rapid growth could not be ignored by the religious leaders among the Sadducees. As a result, the priests ordered the captain of the temple guard to arrest the apostles and put them in jail (Acts 4:1-3). Far from suppressing the growth of the movement, about 5000 from the multitude, who had been listening to the apostles' message, believed and were baptized (4:4). In spite of the persecution, including being flogged at the whipping post, the apostles kept right on preaching and teaching Jesus as the Christ. Nothing short of total conviction and complete dedication to their understanding that this Jesus was truly the Son of God and Savior of humanity could have inspired them to put up with so much abuse.

Caring for Widows and Needy

The rapid growth resulted in some of the widows being overlooked in the daily serving of food (Acts 6:1). Thus, the apostles assembled the congregation and explained that it was not appropriate for them "to neglect the ministry of the word of God in order to wait on tables" (v.2). Consequently, the congregation was to select seven men from their number of good reputation, "full of the Spirit and wisdom" to be put in charge of this task (v.3).

Note how this problem was solved:

> First, the congregation did the selecting of the men, which signified their approval and acceptance of the ones chosen.
>
> Second, the apostles specified the character and quality of the men to be selected. They were to be men with a good reputation, full of the Spirit and of wisdom. Once selected, they "were brought before the apostles who prayed over them and laid their hands on them" (Acts 6:6, NASV). These men were prepared to carry out the task for which they had been chosen.

This occasion raised two issues that needed clarification.

First issue: the care of needs in a church family

In this instance, the apostles were involved fully with preaching the word. Large numbers were responding to the message on a daily basis. Remember, some three thousand were baptized on the first day. Very soon afterwards, another five thousand men heard the message and believed (Acts 4:4). Among this sudden explosion of growth were widows, who were neglected with respect to daily needs. Had this continued, division would have resulted within their ranks. There are times when some things can wait, but this was not one of them. Fortunately, the apostles were quick to recognize the situation and moved with haste to have men selected to meet this need.

Another fact that stands out is that these were Grecian widows fellowshipping with Jewish Christians. It doesn't appear to have been a problem even though it was very soon after Christianity had its beginning. We know that it was a problem at times because the apostle Peter refrained from table fellowship with the Gentiles in Antioch at a considerably later date (Galatians 2:11-14). Even Paul understood that the gospel was first intended to be spread among the Jews. He wrote to the Romans in 1:16, "I am not ashamed of the gospel, because it is the power of God for the salvation of everyone who believes: first for the Jew, then for the Gentile." Perhaps it didn't become a problem in Jerusalem since the apostles were still present among them.

Second issue: the choice of men to serve

In choosing deacons to serve the local church, it is generally agreed that these men constituted the first deacons in the church. Their names appear in Acts 6:5. Stephen—the first mentioned—was a man full of faith and the Holy Spirit. He also is said to be "full of grace and power, and was performing great wonders and signs among the people" (vv. 5-8).

Stephen delivered the message recorded in chapter seven that enraged the men from the Synagogue of the Freedmen to the point that they stoned him to death. In his dying hour, "being full of the Holy Spirit, he gazed intently into heaven and saw the glory of God, and Jesus, standing at the right hand of God" (Acts 7:55, NASV). What a marvelous experience to have as one exits this life for the heavenly realm.

The Selection of Elders

Other than the apostles, who would soon die and pass from the scene, elders (*presbuteroi*) are mentioned first as leaders in the churches. Luke explains that when Paul and Barnabas were returning from their missionary journey in Asia Minor, they appointed elders in every church (Acts 14:23). These appointments probably do not refer to the first selection of elders.

In Acts, chapter fifteen, Luke reports that Paul and Barnabas returned to Jerusalem to receive instructions regarding questions that had arisen in their preaching in Asia Minor. The record states that they went up "to the apostles and elders concerning this issue" (v.2, NASV). This event leads to the conclusion that the first congregation to have elders was the church in Jerusalem, since that is where it all began. Exactly what prompted their appointment and when, is not stated. It is significant to note that the word, "elder," is plural in these verses. Obviously, the position of elder, as a leader among them, was not intended to be filled by only one man. It is important equally to note that in addition to the apostles and elders, the whole church was invited to participate in the choice of the men who were selected (v.22). Experience teaches that people are quicker to support what they help to decide or bring together.

In 1 Peter 5:1, 2, the apostle refers to the elders and identifies their task by saying they are to "shepherd the flock of God *among* you," (v.2, NASV, emphasis added). The shepherd's responsibility is to look after, take care of and provide for his sheep. Notice how Peter words these remarks. The elder's task is to care for the flock that is *among (en humin)* you. The NIV translates this phrase as "under your care," but "among you" is more accurate and is so translated by KJV, ASV, NASV, RSV and Confraternity. It is true that the sheep are under the care of the shepherd, but Peter probably intended his readers to understand that the elders (or shepherd's) responsibility is to move among, that is, serve within the flock. In verse 3, he continues, "not lording it over those in your charge but being examples to the flock." (NASV). Leaders who follow this approach are certain to be the most effective.

In Acts 20:17, Paul was located at Miletus where he invited the elders of the church in Ephesus to join him because he was anxious to arrive in Jerusalem by the day of Pentecost (v.16). He expected this occasion to be his last visit with them. In verse 17, he called them *presbuteroi* - elders. As his admonition and instruction continued, he used the word *episkopous,* translated "overseers," "bishops," "guardians."

> Be on guard for yourselves and for all the flock, among which the Holy Spirit has made you overseers (*episkopous,* plural), to shepherd (*poimeinein*) the church of God which He purchased with His own blood" (v.28, NASV). The NIV changes the infinitive (to shepherd, singular) and translates the remainder of the verse as (Be shepherds of the church of God, which he bought with his own blood (v.28, emphasis added).

For purposes of clarification, please note that the men chosen by the apostles to be leaders, were called *presbuteroi* (tr. elders; Acts 20:17). They were older, mature men, with experience in leadership. Later, in the same context, v.28), Paul refers to them as *episkopous* (bishops, overseers) and *poimenes* (shepherds).

The apostle Peter in his first letter, mentions elders, bishops and shepherds in the first two verses of chapter five and brings it all together.

The effort by some religious groups to make a distinction between elders, bishops and shepherds has no support in Scripture as observed in Acts 20:17, 28; Titus 1:5-8 and 1st Peter 5:1, 2. The word "elder" implies that the person is older and mature in faith; whereas bishop or overseer speaks to his experience in leading, giving direction and being responsible. As shepherd, he feeds, provides for and protects the flock.

In his letter to Timothy, Paul explained the qualifications of the overseers (*episkopoi*) in the first eight verses of chapter three. We know these qualifications are the same for elders since chapter one, verses 5-8 of his letter to Titus uses both elders (*presbuteroi* in v.5) and overseer (*episkopous* in v-7), in spelling out the qualifications.

No super-elders, bishops or shepherds are found in the New Testament's first century churches. Furthermore, there is no evidence in Scripture that one individual served as leader in a single congregation. The choice always involved the appointment of a plurality of men.

Luke recorded that Paul and Barnabas "appointed elders (plural) for them in every church, having prayed with fasting, they commended them to the Lord in whom they had believed" (Acts 14:23, NASV). He also referred to *apostles* and *elders* (note that both words are plural) in the church at Jerusalem (Acts 15:2, 4, 22, 23). Both Peter and James address the entire body of the members assembled to discuss the fact that Gentiles were being converted, but it is James who has the final word. Afterward, the apostles, elders and the whole church choose men from among them to carry the letter they had drafted to the church in Antioch. In that letter, explicit instructions were given regarding how the Gentiles were to be accepted into the fellowship of believers (Acts 15:22-29).

In addition, Paul wrote Titus, instructing him to appoint elders (plural) in every city (Titus 1:5). It seems safe to assume that, at this time, there would have been only one congregation in each city since the missionary effort was so new.

We also know that the church at Philippi had bishops (overseers) because Paul mentioned them in his introductory remarks in Philippians 1:1. Never in Paul's writings is there a reference to only one person as being the leader of any congregation. The appointment of one man as bishop came much later in church history and was the result of failure to follow carefully the teachings found in the New Testament.

Elders were to be family men with one wife and believing children. They were not to be novices or new converts, but were men of age and maturity and each capable of managing his own household well. Paul shows the wisdom in selecting men with these characteristics in 1 Timothy 3 and Titus 1.

The Selection of Deacons

In addition to elders, men known as "deacons" were appointed in every church. Paul mentioned deacons in the Philippian church. When he specified the qualifications of deacons, Paul was careful to state that there was always a plurality of men appointed. This fact appears in the qualifications spelled out in 1 Timothy 3:8-13. The word deacon comes from the Greek, *diakonos,* meaning "servant." Like elders, deacons are to be family men, the husband of one wife, good managers of their children and their own household (1 Timothy 3:8-13).

As mentioned earlier, the position of deacons originated in the Jerusalem church when the Grecian widows were being neglected in "the daily service of food" (Acts 6:1). In any case, their responsibility included providing creature comforts for needy members. In the way that Paul refers to the deacon's qualifications, it obviously was a service rendered only by men since they were said to be the husband of one wife.

The ministry of deacons was not limited solely to acts of service, for Philip, one of the seven chosen in Acts 6:5 to help care for the Grecian widows, is said to have gone "down to the city of Samaria and began proclaiming Christ to them" (Acts 8:5, NASV). Sometime later, an angel of the Lord directed Philip to "Arise and go south to the road that descends from Jerusalem to Gaza" (v.26, NASV), a very deserted area, where he was put in contact with the Ethiopian eunuch, whom he taught and baptized into Christ (Acts 8:27-40). To the extent that we are blessed with spiritual gifts, it stands to reason that the Lord would expect us to make use of them, as Philip did.

Interestingly enough, Paul referred to Phoebe, a sister and servant of the church in Cenchrea (Romans 16:1). The apostle recognized her service to the church and to him as well. True, he called her a *diakanos* (servant) of the church, but he goes no farther—limiting the designation to her life of service and nothing more. There is no indication in the New Testament that women served in any official leadership role.

Self Government

Unlike what is true of many denominations today, no hierarchical arrangement existed in the first century churches. When we look at how things have developed down through the centuries, the self-governing concept makes great sense. Any time one person is put in charge of several congregations there is always greater danger of false teaching permeating the entire group.

Having more than one leader in each church tends to avoid division. If one departs from true teaching, generally the others will bring him around and correct the matter. The likelihood of a plurality of men departing from the truth, all at once, is far less likely to happen. So, having a plurality of men serving as leaders over only one congregation is a safety feature as it relates to unity within the body.

This approach did not rule out cooperation among the churches. Numerous examples exist in the New Testament of churches assisting other churches because of a need. Paul had the Christians at Corinth take up a collection to assist the needy in the church at Jerusalem (1 Corinthians 16:1-4). He further stated that he had directed the churches of Galatia to do likewise (v.1).

The apostle made a point to tell how the Christians at Philippi had sent a gift more than once to supply his needs (Philippians 4:15, 16). So the fact that the churches were independent relating to leadership in no way interfered with their cooperating in matters that helped the church to grow.

A Brief Look At Paul's Life

Before turning to the next subject, it is proper to summarize a few thoughts regarding the apostle Paul. Any careful examination will cause one to conclude that the apostle had a greater impact on Christianity than any of the original twelve apostles, including Peter, John, James and all the others combined. This fact in no way diminishes the work of these men; however, it speaks to the awesome assignment that the Lord expected this outstanding person to fulfill. Here are some of Paul's characteristics and accomplishments:

- He grew up in Tarsus and was exposed to Roman and Greek cultures.
- He was proficient in Greek, Hebrew and possibly Latin.
- He wrote thirteen of the New Testament books. If Hebrews is attributed to the apostle, that would account for more than one-half of the entire New Testament.
- He addressed every major issue of the day, including slavery, race, marriage, homosexuality, Gnosticism and unity and did not hesitate to debate the highly educated theologians and philosophers. He kept a clear conscience and spoke the truth with love.
- He traveled hundreds, possibly thousands of miles by land and sea, on foot, donkey, camel and ship to share the gospel of Christ.

The apostle stated his purpose for ministry with these words:

> Though I am free and belong to no man, I make myself a slave to everyone, to win as many as possible.... I have become all things to all men so that by all possible means I might save some (1 Corinthians 9:19-22b).

In his second letter to Timothy, Paul summarizes the entire story with the following quotation. "The Lord will rescue me from every evil attack and will bring me safely to his *heavenly kingdom*. To him be the glory for ever and ever. Amen" (2 Timothy 4:18, emphasis added).

The Seven Churches of Asia

Jesus' letters to the seven churches of Asia Minor recorded by John in the Book of Revelation are unique. They are somewhat similar to Paul's teaching in that each letter is addressed to a church in a specific location (for example, Ephesus). Beyond this, there are some definite and unique distinctions. To begin, each letter was addressed to the angel of the church. English versions translate the word, *angelos*, as "angel" although it can be rendered "messenger." The message delivered to the angel is from "one like a son of man" (Revelation 1:13), and can be none other than Jesus Christ. In the letter to Thyatira, he refers to this "One" as "The Son of God" (2:18b). No church other than the seven to whom John writes is addressed through its angel.

If "angel" is the correct translation, then the angel would need to become like a human being to communicate with Christians in each congregation. However, to translate *angelos* as "messenger" still raises questions. Who is this messenger? Some have suggested that he is a leader in the congregation. That cannot be ruled out, but it has nothing in common with the organization found in churches throughout the New Testament in other locations. For example, the church in Jerusalem had elders. Congregations started by Paul and Barnabas had elders, (Acts 14:23).

We know that Paul visited Ephesus, and on one occasion spent two years teaching in the school of Tyrannus (Acts 19:10). Early in this journey, he met with some disciples at Ephesus who had been taught by Apollos (Acts 18:24), but knew nothing about the Holy Spirit—a problem that Paul took time to correct (Acts 19:1-5). The apostle's work in the School of Tyrannus prompted Luke to write, "all the Jews and Greeks who lived in the province of Asia heard the word of the Lord" (Acts 19:10).

It is possible that more than one congregation existed in Ephesus, and if this assumption is true, it may explain why the churches John addressed, including Ephesus, did not mention elders and deacons. We do know from other readings that Paul made the effort to appoint elders rather soon after establishing a congregation (Acts 14:21-23).

Tradition holds that John was forced to leave this area of Asia Minor to live out the remainder of his life on the island of Patmos where there is a grave site at the top of the hill that supposedly contains the apostle's remains. This assumption, however, is rejected by some who have studied carefully the evidence.

Considering the way the message spread from the School of Tyrannus, John certainly must have been familiar with some of these churches. His letter to the church at Ephesus gives reason to conclude that it had existed for a considerable period of time, including the events of Acts, chapter nineteen. If this observation is accurate, it does raise questions as to why the churches are addressed through an angel.

It is possible that, since the Lord had John address the Revelation letter by means of apocalyptic language, he uses the word *angel* to confuse enemies of the churches who sought to destroy them. The book is filled with symbolisms for a good reason. It is interesting that angels are incorporated into the message throughout the book.

Finally, there is the concluding remark to each church that "hears what the Spirit says to the churches." This statement may be a thought unique with John, who intended to emphasize the work of the Spirit. The Holy Spirit, the author of the word, uses the minds and hands of human beings to deliver the message. In any case, nothing is said about elders and deacons in these seven churches. Only the angel of each church is mentioned.

Summary

> Three examples show how the first century Christians handled disagreements. Paul first dealt with the division in the church at Corinth. Then he considered the problem at Rome (chapter 14) that arose between new converts and mature Christians. The third example looked at the problem of circumcision.
>
> The name by which churches have been recognized for generations has been changed.
>
> Rapid growth in the early church required careful organization for the church to go forward. Men called *deacons* were appointed in every church to serve according to their need.
>
> Each congregation received oversight by its own governing body of elders and deacons.
>
> The seven churches of Asia are unique in the way they are addressed by the apostle John.

Chapter twelve makes a plea for Christians to be united in our core values. Division diminishes our efforts to share the Good News with people who do not know God and Jesus Christ as Lord, Savior and Redeemer.

Jesus knew that Satan's most effective weapon was his ability to promote division among his disciples; consequently, he inspired the apostle John to devote the entire seventeenth chapter of the fourth gospel to an appeal for unity.

“Love One Another As I Have Loved You”

Jesus left these words with his twelve chosen disciples to assure them this would be the test used by people to determine if they truly were his disciples (John 13:34, 35).

So much is said about people faking things today, but there was no mistaking how Jesus applied the test. He took a basin of water and a towel and washed the disciples feet.

When he had finished washing their feet, he asked: “Do you understand what I have done for you?”... “You call me ‘Teacher’ and ‘Lord’ and rightly so, for that is what I am....I have set you an example that you should do as I have done for you’” (John 13:12-15).

We learn Best from Example.

Chapter 12

Appeal for Unity

If the religious world is ever able to come together and be united as one body, it will be the result of our loving one another in the manner described by Jesus a short time before his crucifixion. He gave a "new command" to his disciples, instructing that they must love one another as he had loved them. He further indicated that the world would come to recognize them as his followers if they demonstrated genuine love for one another (John13:34).

To the teacher of the law who inquired about the most important commandment, Jesus responded: "Hear, O Israel, the Lord our God, the Lord is one. Love the Lord your God with all your heart and with all your soul and with all your mind and with all your strength" (Mark 12: 29, 30). In other words, God is to be loved with our entire being. Our love for God must take priority over everything else and everyone else.

During the last supper before his trial, Jesus showed his disciples "the full extent of his love" (John 13:1), when he took a towel and washed their feet. Having finished, he declared that they should do for one another as he had done for them (vv. 14, 15). Afterward, he followed with the crowning thought:

> A new command I give you: Love one another. As I have loved you, so you must love one another. By this

> all men will know that you are my disciples, if you love one another (vv. 34, 35).

In the apostle John's first epistle, he devotes the majority of chapters three through five to the discussion of love. The emphasis in chapter three is on loving one another. To help us grasp the true meaning of love, John follows with the example of Jesus Christ laying down his life for the human race. Of course, no greater love can exist than that shown by Jesus. But John, who is referred to as "the disciple whom Jesus loved" (John 21:20), has more to say regarding this matter. He illustrates his point by describing an individual who has been blessed abundantly with material possessions. A poor brother in the church is in need, and his circumstance is known by a wealthy brother, yet he does nothing to alleviate the need. The apostle's answer framed as a question really stings: "...how can the love of God be in him?" (3:17). The point is that loving with words and the tongue apart from actions and deeds fails the test. Our love is measured by the way we live, serve and obey God's commands.

John then writes, "There is no fear in love. But perfect love drives out fear, because fear has to do with punishment" (4:18). The apostle's use of the words "fear" and "love" are framed within the context of our relationship with God and eternal life. Fear in other realms (for example, fear of falling from extreme heights) has nothing to do with love. As for "perfect love," the number of Christians who qualify probably drops close to zero, but "perfect love" provides the standard toward which we should be aiming.

Both John, in the preceding context, and Paul in 1 Corinthians 13 uses the word *agape* to identify love. "Agape" defined—presents love in its loftiest, most genuine form and is expressed toward another person without regard to any thought of being returned in kind or at all. It manifests itself in deed and truth.

It takes the pen of the apostle Paul to enlarge our understanding of what Biblical love truly involves. In his first letter to the Corinthian Church, he devoted what presently includes an entire chapter to understanding love. Chapter thirteen opens using words of lofty eloquence. "If I speak in the tongues of men and of angels, but have not love, I am only a resounding gong or a clanging cymbal." To put it in other words, one could be the greatest orator that ever lived, but failing to possess genuine love, it would accomplish nothing more than a noisy bag of wind.

I could be a prophetic genius with knowledge to explain mysterious events, but failing to exercise agape love in the process would amount to nothing. Possessing faith that would remove mountains, but failing to perform this great act without love would earn me nothing more than a great big zero. Even if I gave all my possessions to care for the poor, and in the process my body was consumed by flames of fire, yet failed to possess love in the act, it would gain me nothing. In other words, the greatest, most wonderful act of service rendered apart from love makes no contribution to my eternal wellbeing.

What Defines Love?

Starting with verse four, the apostle begins to explain how *love* is recognized:

> Paul declares love...
> ... is — patient, kind, keeps no record of wrongs, rejoices with the truth.
> ... always — protects, trusts, hopes, perseveres.
> ...is — not proud, rude, self-seeking, easily angered.
> ...does — not envy, boast, delight in evil.
> ...never — fails.

Paul concludes by pointing out that the time will come when prophetic utterances will cease; speaking in tongues will be silenced and knowledge will pass away. Even faith and hope will have accomplished their role in our spiritual development and will cease to function. Not so, with love! Since God is love, and He admonishes us to emulate that love—an affectionate outpouring of agape love will constantly flow from our eternal spirits toward our heavenly Father, once we have passed from the physical realm into the spiritual.

That They All Be One

It comes as no surprise that Jesus, in preparation for his departure from this world and ascension to the Father in heaven, would fervently pray for the apostles to remain united as one. The entire seventeenth chapter of John's gospel is devoted to unity. Jesus prayed for the Father to keep his disciples in His name "so that they may be one as we are one" (John 17:11). He continues by saying that while he was with them he kept and securely guarded them from the evil one. Only Judas, the son of perdition, forsook him—a fact that was prophesied in Scripture.

It is significant that Jesus repeated many times the importance of the disciples holding to the truth he had shared with them. This perfect unity would serve to help convince others of the Father's love and purpose in sending Jesus. How different this world would be if all who profess to follow Jesus would unite as one body and accept the truth taught in Scripture!

It is sad that the twelve disciples whom Jesus chose to begin the task of carrying his message to the world often were poor examples relating to unity. Matthew records the incident of the mother of James and John coming to Jesus and requesting that they be allowed to take a seat, one on his right and the other on his left in his kingdom. Jesus reminded them that this request was not his to give. We are told that when the ten heard this request, they became indignant at the two brothers.

This mother's request provided a teaching opportunity for the Lord. He explained how the rulers of the Gentiles lorded it over some, and the great men among them exercised authority over them

(Matthew 20:24-27). He expected better behavior from his disciples by saying: "It is not so among you, but whoever wishes to become great among you shall be your servant. And whoever wishes to be first among you shall be your slave" (vv. 26, 27). He continued by referring to himself as the appropriate example of proper behavior in these words: "Just as the Son of man did not come to be served, but to serve, and to give his life a ransom for many" (v.28). Did they get the message? One would have to conclude, *"not completely,"* based on future happenings.

The Scribes and Pharisees and other religious leaders missed the point of unity and serving others. Jesus explained how they scrambled to occupy "the chair of Moses" (Matthew 23:2), but made little effort to follow his teaching. He accused them of saying one thing and doing another. Furthermore, they performed their deeds to impress people, not to please God. It is similar behavior that contributes to a large degree to so much religious division in today's world.

Jesus' teaching on unity also reminds us of the problem with which Paul was confronted in the city of Corinth. He began by emphasizing God's faithfulness, and how they have been called into fellowship with his Son, Jesus Christ (1 Corinthians 1:9). Next, he exhorted them in the name of the Lord Jesus Christ to agree and not be divided. This teaching required their being complete in the same mind and the same judgment (v.10).

Why was it necessary for the apostle to begin his letter with this strong admonition regarding the need for unity? Chloe's household had reported to Paul that the church members were quarreling, and complaining regarding core issues. As was mentioned earlier, some members identified with Paul, some with Apollos, some with Cephas and others with Christ. The tempo must have reached the boiling point with disagreeing Christians ready to explode.

Disagreements of this magnitude have led to divisions down through the ages causing multitudes of sincere, searching people to turn away and refuse to give Christianity an honest appraisal. Usually, what is said by unbelievers is, "If that is Christianity, then I don't want any part of it." Unfortunately, there is usually little we can do to reverse such reaction. As the late brother Otis Gatewood once observed: "Anything presented in the objective case and the kickative mood is seldom favorably received by the one listening."

Paul, a Constant Advocate for Unity

A careful study of the apostle Paul's letters compels us to conclude that no one devoted greater energy to the plea for unity, than did the Lord himself. In his letter to the Ephesian Christians, Paul devoted the entire fourth chapter to addressing the manner of their calling and how it affects their unity. He began by making an appeal (i.e., entreating them) to live in a manner worthy of their calling. They were encouraged to manifest a humble nature, a gentle spirit, and a patient attitude that bears with one another in love (vv. 1, 2). Such behavior certainly always will contribute to a harmonious situation. The word, *spudazo*, implies "zeal," "eagerness" or as the NIV renders it, "Make every effort to keep the unity of the Spirit through the bond of peace" (v. 3). It is more accurate to translate this last phrase "in the bond of peace." These admonitions are an introduction to what he really wants to emphasize beginning with Ephesians 4:4.

Most translations begin this verse with "There is one body." However, Paul simply stated: "...one body and one Spirit, just as also you were called in one hope of your calling; one Lord, one faith, one baptism, one God and Father of all who is over all and through all and in all" (vv. 4-6, my translation). Observe that Paul lists seven "ones." The number seven implies perfection. In each case, there is only "one." Notice the importance of each of these "one" characteristics:

(1) There is One Body.

We are not left to guess about the body, since the apostle declares the body to be the church of which Christ is the head and savior

(Ephesians 5:23). In chapter 4:11, 12, he lists as part of the church—apostles, prophets, evangelists, pastors and teachers—and describes their works as being that of "building up of the body of Christ." He repeats the "one body" concept a number of times in 1 Corinthians 12, and declares it to be the church" (v. 28). Unfortunately, the "one body" (i.e., "one church") teaching, like so many other teachings on the church found in Scripture, has been ignored totally by the religious world.

(2) There Is One Spirit.

Paul's "one spirit" can only refer to the Holy Spirit. In 1 Corinthians 12:13, he writes: "For by one Spirit we were all baptized into one body whether Jews or Greeks, whether slaves or free, and we were all made to drink of one Spirit."

Jesus told his apostles that the Father would send the Holy Spirit in his name to "teach you all things, and bring to your remembrance all that I said to you" (John 14:26). The Spirit is also called "Counselor" ("Helper" in the NASV) in this verse. In John 15:26, Jesus calls the Holy Spirit "Counselor" and "Spirit of truth." In chapter sixteen, Jesus told these men that he would send the Holy Spirit, who would convict the world of "sin, righteousness and judgment" (v.8). He further stated that when "the Spirit of truth, comes, he will guide you into all truth" (v.13).

To Christians at Corinth, Paul wrote: "Or do you not know that your body is a temple of the Holy Spirit who is in you, whom you have from God?" (1 Corinthians 6:19). Of the seven men chosen to care for the Hellenistic widows in Jerusalem, Luke states that Stephen was a man, "full of faith and the Holy Spirit" (Acts 6:5). In chapter five, Peter and the apostles answered the Jewish council with these words: "And we are witnesses of these things, and so is the Holy Spirit, whom God has given to those who obey Him" (5:32). Soon after Paul's conversion, while he was still known as Saul, we read: "So the church throughout all Judea and Galilee and Samaria enjoyed peace, being built up; and, going on in the fear of the Lord and in the comfort of the Holy Spirit, it continued to increase" (Acts 9:31, NASV).

The Holy Spirit is active both in an individual and collective manner in the churches. It is the same Spirit—the "one Spirit"—that Paul describes and urges the Christians not to "grieve…with whom you were sealed for the day of redemption" (Ephesians 4:4, 30).

(3) You Were Called in One Hope of Your Calling

Hope, as it is used in the New Testament, relates to our salvation and portrays assurance and certainty. When the apostle Paul was making his defense before Felix, the governor, he stated that his confidence in God caused him to have a hope that "there will be a resurrection of both the righteous and the wicked" (Acts 24:15). There is never a doubt in the apostle's mind regarding the resurrection.

In his letter to the Christians at Colossae, Paul expressed his thankfulness for their faith in Christ Jesus and their love for all the saints. He further indicated that this (their faith and love) assures "the hope laid up for you in heaven, of which you previously heard in the word of truth, the gospel" (Colossians 1:4, 5). They had been introduced to heavenly citizenship from the good news of the gospel that Paul and his companions had taught them.

In the introductory comment of the apostle's letter to Titus, he made reference to his "hope of eternal life, which God, who cannot lie, promised long ages ago" (Titus 1:2). We know that God cannot lie; therefore, the reality of eternal life is as certain as are the promises of God. Farther along in the letter he declared, "This is a trustworthy statement: and concerning these things I want you to speak confidently" (Titus 3:8). In the previous verse, he stated that we are justified by God's grace and are "made heirs according to the hope of eternal life." To be sure, there is one hope of our calling that ends in eternal life with God.

(4)There *is One Lord*

The word "Lord" is used many times in the Old Testament, usually referring to God, as in Genesis 17:1 which reads: "Now when Abram was ninety-nine years old, the Lord appeared to Abram and said to him, 'I am God Almighty; Walk before Me and be blameless" (NASV). The one expression that is repeated hundreds of times begins in Exodus 4:2, 4, "The Lord said to Moses;" and continues through the book of Deuteronomy. At times it refers to a dignitary such as King Nebuchadnezzar when Daniel was interpreting his dream. It reads, "this is the decree of the Most High, which has come on my Lord the king" (Daniel 4:24). Although the word "Lord" is sometimes used to designate God in the New Testament, in Ephesians 4:5 it definitely is referring to Jesus Christ. Of this interpretation we can be certain because verse six begins with, "one God and Father of all." So, there is only one Lord Jesus Christ.

Paul frequently uses the expression "God and Father of our Lord Jesus Christ" (Romans 1:7; 1 Corinthians 1:2, 3; Ephesians 1:3; Colossians 1:2). These or similar words are used as introductory comments in almost every letter Paul wrote. James, Peter and Jude also use expressions almost identical to Paul's use in the beginning of their letters.

Occasionally, all three members of the Godhead appear together as in 2 Corinthians 13:14, where he concludes: "The grace of the Lord Jesus Christ, and the love of God, and the fellowship of the Holy Spirit, be with you all."

(5) There Is One Faith

Most commentators think that Paul is referring to the Christian system of doctrine, not to one's personal faith. However, William Hendricksen, in his analysis of Paul's letter to the Ephesians, disagrees with "most commentators," arguing that "faith" refers to personal faith because "one faith" follows the "one Lord" statement and comes before "one baptism," indicating a close knit unit."[5]

My personal view is in agreement with those who take it to be referring to the Christian system.

(6) There Is One Baptism

There are seven different baptisms mentioned in the New Testament; consequently, it is important to study the apostle Paul's inspired explanation of the "one baptism." This *one baptism* obviously pertains to our present Christian life, and is to be practiced until the end of the age. The *one baptism* is mentioned by Jesus both in Matthew 28:19, 20 and Mark 16:15, 16 when the two writers record the Great Commission given by the Lord near the end of his ministry. Matthew states:

"Therefore go and make disciples of all nations, *baptizing them* in the name of the Father and of the Son and of the Holy Spirit," (v.19, emphasis added).

- Mark states:

  Go into all the world and preach the good news to all creation. Whoever believes and is *baptized* will be saved, but whoever does not believe will be condemned (vv. 15, 16, emphasis added).

This baptism was to take place following the preaching of the Gospel, and its acceptance by the candidate (Acts 2:37-38 and Acts 10:47-48).

In Romans 1:16, Paul explains that the Gospel would first be presented to the Jews and later, to the Gentiles. In Acts chapter two, the audience consists of Jews. In chapter ten, the audience is the household of Cornelius, who are Gentiles.

(7) There Is One God and Father of All

- Everything has its beginning with God. The book of Genesis opens by introducing the Creator with these words: "In the beginning God created the heavens and the earth" (Genesis 1:1). It is true that the word *Elohim* (translated "God" in English,) is plural; however, it is a reference to the one deity. We know this interpretation to be true because the verb, *bara,* that follows is translated "created" and is singular.

Paul, in writing to the young man Timothy, declared: "For there is one God, and one mediator also between God and men, the man Christ Jesus" (1Timothy 2:5).

"All things" began with God and all will conclude with God. Nothing can be eliminated from this list of "all things," if unity is to be achieved today in our religious world.

Applying the Golden Rule

If ever there is unity in the Christian world, it will be a result of applying what is referred to as *the golden rule,* which Jesus declared: "So in everything, do to others what you would have them do to you, for this sums up the Law and the Prophets" (Matthew 7:12). This wonderful principle covers every aspect of our relationships together. Every normal person realizes that if we treat others in the same way we desire to be treated, only good things will be the result.

It is no surprise that the apostle Paul accomplished so much during his ministry among the Gentiles. The secret of his success is summarized in his letter to the Christians at Ephesus.

> Let all bitterness and wrath and anger and clamor and slander be put away from you, along with all malice. And be kind to one another, tender-hearted,

> forgiving each others, just as God in Christ also has forgiven you (Ephesians 4:31, 32).

Any reasonable person would want to bury the negative behaviors of "bitterness, wrath, anger, clamor and slander." In their place, Paul gave positive behaviors that are achievable in a Christian's life:

- *"Kindness"* is a virtue appreciated by young and old, wealthy and poor, intelligent and ignorant, weak and strong—in short, everyone. Practicing this principle will bring out the best in every individual and will promote tranquility and harmony among all who cherish peace. Not only does it work wonders within the human family, it is equally appreciated in the animal kingdom. Important as kindness is, we don't always see it practiced among people who claim to be *followers* of the Lord Jesus Christ. To get along and live in a harmonious way, kindness is an important virtue.
- *"Tender heart"* is mentioned after kindness. The two fit together naturally like a glove and hand. A *tender heart* produces *kindness*, and together they bring out the best in people. Both are important for achieving unity.
- *"Forgiving one another."* Nothing destroys marriages more than unwillingness to forgive when offenses occur between husbands and wives. When a husband or wife is offended or hurt by something the other has said or done, invariably the offended party is unable to forget it. This, too often, happens even though an apology is offered to make it right. Consequently, the next time a disagreement surfaces, the offended party brings up the old issue and will use it to punish the other party. This behavior will in time drive a wedge between husband and wife that cannot be removed. Not only will this type of situation destroy a marriage but it divides family members, friends, and other relationships. It also can

> divide a church, which is why Paul is emphasizing *forgive one another* to the Corinthians.

The basis for practicing forgiveness is rooted in the realization that God has arranged through the gift of his Son, Jesus Christ, to forgive us. Jesus included this thought in his model prayer: "Forgive us our debts, as we also have forgiven our debtors" (Matthew 6:12). In verses 14 and 15, he stated the reason for forgiveness:

> For if you forgive men when they sin against you, your heavenly Father will also forgive you. But if you do not forgive men their sins, your Father will not forgive your sins.

If we expect our heavenly Father to forgive our shortcomings and failures that constitute sin, we must forgive those who sin against us. Granted that is strong teaching, which is difficult to put into practice, but its application to personal and church divisions make it very important to master and apply.

In discussing repentance and forgiveness with the disciples, Jesus made a statement that relates to forgiveness: "Be on your guard! If your brother sins, rebuke him, and if he repents, forgive him" (Luke 17:3, NASV). In this instance, the Lord places a condition on both parties. However, some commentators believe that it is better for the offended individual to forgive even if the offending individual is unwilling to repent and correct the violation. Perhaps for one's own satisfaction and peace of mind, this interpretation of Jesus' model prayer may be true, but such a response is not required by the teaching contained in Luke's passage.

Paul's admonitions on peace and harmony

Paul's letter to the Christians at Rome is a masterpiece in dealing with problems that arise within families and among individuals. Applying his admonitions given in chapters eight and twelve will mold one's attitude in the direction of living in unity, harmony and peace with fellow human beings. Note his teaching:

- ✓ Romans 8:1: Our victory over sin and death is found in Christ Jesus because "there is now no condemnation for those who are in Christ Jesus."
- ✓ Romans 8:28: God causes "all things to work together for good for those who love Him and are called according to His purpose."
- ✓ Romans 8:38, 39: Paul declares that "nothing can separate us from the love of God, which is in Christ Jesus our Lord." He enumerates a list of "nothings" that lack power to "separate us from the love of God, which is in Christ Jesus our Lord:" "Neither death, nor life, nor angels, nor principalities, nor things present, nor things to come, nor powers, nor height, nor depth nor any other created thing."
- ✓ Romans 12:9-21: Paul's list of short, quick-hitting statements is a good guidepost to right living. Immerse yourself in these beautiful expressions. They will change emotions, grip the heart and transform lives for the better.

Maintaining Peace While Settling Differences

The New Testament is the world's best manual for keeping peace and resolving differences among people. For example, the apostle Paul in Romans chapter fourteen, outlines ways to heal differences between Christians—ways that are good patterns to follow in any conflict. In this instance, the conflict that is dividing the church involves food that is acceptable for Christians to eat when it comes from idol worship. While this conflict is not one that would divide people today, the model for resolving differences is applicable to any dispute that destroys unity.

Paul begins by contrasting the faith of two people: one whose faith allows him to eat anything, while the other Christian who is weak in faith limits his personal menu to eating vegetables and condemns eating meat offered to idols. The background of the dispute, then, focuses on sacrifices offered in pagan temples and later sold in the open meat-market. The mature Christian could purchase this meat, prepare it and eat it conscientiously. On the other hand, the person weak in faith considered this act to be sin.

The apostle approaches this subject as being a matter of dispute and withholds his personal judgment as he helps the two parties to find a solution that will keep the peace within the congregation. The conflict is generated because the person whose maturity in faith allows him to eat anything, but his brother who is weak in faith cannot eat this meat and is limited to vegetables? While this is a "strong Christian"-"weak Christian" problem, Paul's solution, inspired by the Holy Spirit, is a model for solving most disagreements in the church:

- Although the mature brother's conscience permits him to eat the meat, he must not look down on (the Greek word, exouqenew, can be translated "to look down on, despise, disdain, reject or regard with contempt") the "weak Christian."
- The "weak Christian," who does not eat everything, must not condemn (the Greek word, krinetw, means "to condemn, find fault with, criticize, pass an unfavorable judgment upon") the brother who does.
- Paul suggests a solution based on the premise that God accepts both men without condemning them. The fact that God accepts them is sufficient reason for both brothers, and the church, to accept and fellowship each other. The result

of this acceptance means that our worship assemblies will be uplifting for all Christians without disagreements and public debates. No "sides" will be drawn nor arguments for and against be made in the assembly.

- Paul gives the same reason for his decision: both brothers do "so to the Lord and gives thanks to God" (v.6-b).
- It is not our place to judge another's servant. The other person is not our servant. Paul adds: "To his own master he stands or falls. And he will stand, for the Lord is able to make him stand" (Romans 14:4). The Lord is our master, not some human being.

In this context the apostle brings up another point by way of illustrating how such matters should be settled. It deals with how we differentiate regarding days. "One man considers one day more sacred than another; another man considers every day alike" (v.5). The solution is found in applying the principle to eating meat. There is precious little that cannot be resolved by applying the above principle.

One additional point is covered in verses 12-23 that is extremely important. We are not to put a stumbling block or obstacle in another Christian's way. As a Christian who is in the Lord, Paul understands that no food is unclean in itself, which means that he is free to eat anything. However, the apostle declares that he would refrain from eating meat, drinking wine or doing anything else that would cause a brother to stumble or fall away (vv. 20, 21).

Finally, pay careful attention to the following, noting the emphasis added to the verses:

> Let us therefore *make every effort* to do what *leads to peace and to mutual edification*...So whatever you believe about these things *keep between yourself and God* (vv. 19, 22, emphasis added).

Peter's admonitions on unity and harmony

The apostle Peter in his first letter also included many thoughts regarding relationships that contribute to unity and peace:

1 Peter 1:14-21: As obedient children, we are admonished to be holy like the Holy One (referring to Jesus Christ) who called us to put our faith and hope in God.

I Peter 1: 22,23: Since we have been "born again" of imperishable seed—the living and abiding word of God—we are to love one another fervently from the heart.

I Peter 3:8, 9: Peter sums up the place of love in unity: "Finally, all of you, live in harmony with one another; be sympathetic, love as brothers, be compassionate and humble. Do not repay evil with evil or insult with insult, but with blessing, because to this you were called so that you may inherit a blessing."

I Peter 4:8: Above all, keep fervent in your love for one another, because love covers a multitude of sins. "The word for love is *agape,* which describes the deepest, most compelling expression emanating from the inner being. Following his admonition "to keep fervent in our love" he continues: "Be hospitable to one another without complaint. As each one has received a special gift, employ it in serving one another, as good servants of the manifold grace of God (4:9,10). As to our speech and service, he continues that it should always be done to glorify God through Jesus Christ (4:11).

A careful reading of Peter's entire letter will uncover numerous other gems that are helpful in achieving unity. In his second letter, he concludes with this admonition: "But grow in the grace and knowledge of our Lord and Savior Jesus Christ. To Him be the glory, both now and to the day of eternity" (2 Peter 3:18). Two important words are embedded in this verse:

- *Grace*: the unmerited favor given by God through Jesus Christ that we in no way deserve. Stated as an acrostic—which means that each letter of a word is the first letter of another word—"Grace" becomes ***G****od's* ***R****iches* ***A****t* ***C****hrist's* ***E****xpense.* The acrostic emphasizes that God willingly permitted His Son, Jesus Christ, to suffer the agony of death on Calvary's cross to atone for our sins.
- *Knowledge*: The more we learn and emulate in our lives regarding the life of Jesus, the easier it will be to live in harmony and peace with our fellow human beings.

To wrap up this section, you are urged to turn to Matthew, chapters five through seven, and study carefully and prayerfully the teaching of Jesus, commonly referred to as *The Sermon on the Mount.* No one ever has come close to composing these goals for living. They call us to life on the highest plane. To completely live by them would eliminate poverty, hunger, war and all forms of evil.

Summary

One of the longest prayers spoken by Jesus to his Father, recorded in the New Testament, focuses on the need for unity among the twelve apostles. His appeal was for them to be one just as he and the Father were one.

> Jesus knew that people of the world would evaluate their love for him and the Father in keeping with the manner in which they loved one another.
>
> He (Jesus) declared that love for God must encompass the whole person—heart, soul, mind and strength—including love for one's neighbor.
>
> Both John and Paul went to great lengths to describe how the love of God will mold us so we can be victorious in living the Christian life. Paul contrasted faith, hope and love but ended by declaring that only love will continue forever, even in heaven.
>
> The apostle continued by describing the seven "ones:" one *body,* one *Spirit,* one *hope,* one *Lord,* one *faith,* one *baptism,* one *God* and Father of all.
>
> Quotations from the writings of both Paul and Peter covering unity, harmony, peace and agape love are included in this chapter.
>
> Maintaining peace while settling differences is discussed near the end of the chapter.

Chapter 13 deals with how we transition from this life to eternal life in heaven, and ends with an appeal for the reader to join us in a life of worship and service consistent with what Jesus and the New Testament writers provide as an example to follow.

The Choice Is Ours

The invitation of Jesus reads: "Come to me, all you who are weary and burdened, and I will give you rest. Take my yoke upon you and learn from me, for I am gentle and humble in heart, and you will find rest for your souls. For my yoke is easy and my burden is light" (Matthew 11:28-30).

Jesus came to give us abundant life here and now (John 10:10), and eternal life in heaven. This world is not the Christian's permanent home.

Our resurrection and eternal life in heaven are arranged through Jesus Christ. Here is how the apostle Paul worded it:

Forgetting what is behind...I press on toward the goal to win the prize for which God has called me heavenward in Christ Jesus (Philippians 3:13, 14).

CHAPTER 13

The Ultimate Reward, Eternal Life in Heaven

The purpose of this chapter is twofold: (a) to admonish us to make heaven our eternal goal and (b) to reemphasize the urgent need for today's Christians to unite in our effort to reach the lost with the amazing story of salvation.

To begin, we are given a choice. God has created us with free will and admonishes us to choose *life* through Jesus Christ. No one is forced to love and serve Him, but to reject His invitation will be tragic.

- ✓ We can choose to go with God and be given eternal life, or
- ✓ We can choose to reject God and suffer eternal punishment.

The same Bible that describes *heaven* with all of its glory and beauty explains the horrors of everlasting punishment. (Matthew 25:31-46). The thought of continuous fire gives reason to cringe with fear.

We can be assured that the God who created us has no desire that a single one miss the goal of heaven and end up in torment. John, the apostle of love, described how God, our heavenly Father, arranged for His one and only unique Son, Jesus Christ, to come to this earth and sacrifice his life on Calvary's cross to atone for our sins. In so doing,

He provided the way for us to enjoy the abundant life here and now, and ultimately eternal life in heaven (John 3:16; 10:10).

Our Resurrection And Eternal Life Are Obtained Only Through Jesus

When the Lord was consoling Martha and Mary, two of his dear friends, regarding the death of their brother Lazarus, he explained that their brother would rise again. Martha responded, "'I know he will rise again in the resurrection at the last day'" (John 11:24).

Regarding death, resurrection, and the end of the age, Martha was correct.

> However, Jesus' answer was somewhat confusing to her. He replied:
>
> 'I am the resurrection and the life. He who believes in me will live, even though he dies; and whoever lives and believes in me, will never die. Do you believe this?' (vv. 25, 26).

Her answer: "'Yes Lord.... I believe you are the Christ, the Son of God, who was to come into the world'" (v.27). What wasn't completely clear to Martha was that the Lord was talking about both physical and spiritual life and death. Lazarus was physically dead, but Jesus knew that he would be returning to physical life in a moment. His resurrected, spiritual body would come to life during the final resurrection at the judgment day when time was no more.

The apostles, John and Paul described how everything is to conclude once the Lord's work is completed fully upon the earth.

In describing death and the resurrection to follow, Paul wrote the following to the Christians at Philippi: "For to me, to live is Christ and to die is gain.... I desire to depart and be with Christ, which is better by far" (Philippians 1:21,23). The apostle understood that death meant going home to be with the Lord in heaven, forever. If, however, remaining with them temporarily would lead to their progress and joy in Christ Jesus, then he was ready to do that.

Paul definitely had a goal in mind on which he kept his eyes focused and his thoughts centered, daily. Take note how he expressed it:

> Brothers, I do not consider myself yet to have taken hold of it. But one thing I do: Forgetting what is behind and straining toward what is ahead, I press on toward the goal to win the prize for which God has called me heavenward in Christ Jesus (Philippians 3:13,14).

He dealt extensively with this event in letters to the Christians in Corinth and Thessalonica.

First Letter to Corinth

The question was being raised by some of the Christians in Corinth regarding what happens at death. Some were saying there was no such thing as resurrection of the dead (1 Corinthians 15:12-19). To refute this comment, the apostle used the example of Jesus Christ. The fact that Jesus rose from the dead three days after being buried in the tomb could not be denied. So, to reason that the dead are not raised would contradict the obvious message spoken by the angel to the women: "I know that you are looking for Jesus, who was crucified. He is not here; he has risen, just as he said. Come and see the place where he lay" (Matthew 28:5, 6).

In addition, the apostle had personally shared with them what he considered to be of first importance,

> that Christ died for our sins according to the Scriptures, that he was buried, that he was raised on the third day according to the Scriptures, and that he

> appeared to *Peter,* and then to the *Twelve.* After that, he appeared to *more than five hundred of the brothers* at the same time, most of whom are still living, though some have fallen asleep. Then he appeared to *James,* then to *all the apostles,* and last of all he appeared to *me* also, as to one abnormally born (1 Corinthians 15:3-8, emphasis added).

To deny this fact, Paul stated, was to render their preaching useless, their faith futile, leaving them still in their sins, lost and without hope (15:14-19). He added: "Come back to your senses as you ought, and stop sinning" (v. 34).

His next point reads:

> For since death came through a man, the resurrection of the dead comes also through a man. For as *in Adam all die,* so *in Christ all will be made alive.* But each in his own turn: Christ, the firstfruits; then, when he comes, those who belong to him. Then *the end will come,* when he hands over the kingdom to God the Father after he has destroyed all dominion, authority and power (15:21-24, emphasis added).

Four important facts are included in Pau's writing:

(1) Paul states that death came through a man, *Adam,* and resurrection from the dead will come through *Jesus Christ.*
(2) The order will be Christ first, who constitutes the *first fruits* of the resurrection. Then, when he comes, those who belong to him will follow. Paul's statement, "*those who belong to him,*" refers to the Lord's faithful ones.
(3) This event will be followed by the end of this world.

(4) When the end occurs, Christ Jesus will relinquish his reign and hand over the kingdom to the Father "so that God may be all in all" (1 Corinthians 15:28).

In describing our resurrected body, the apostle anticipated two questions:

(1) "How are the dead raised?" (2) "With what kind of body will they come?" He answered by first explaining that this physical body will perish at death and return to the earth because "flesh and blood cannot inherit the kingdom of God" (1 Corinthians 15:50). Paul answers the second question by stating that our mortal, perishable body will become an imperishable, immortal body suitable for heaven.

Think of it: he is describing a body that does not grow old, that will not wear out, but continues in a state of perfection forever!

Second Letter to Thessalonians

Paul writes—regarding the coming of Jesus—that Christians in Thessalonica had received instruction regarding times and dates of the Lord's return. The reality is that no one knows. Matthew quotes Jesus as saying: "'*No one knows* about that day or hour, not even the angels in heaven, nor the Son, but *only the Father*'" (Matthew 24:36, emphasis added). It really is not important for us to know the exact date. In fact, it is best that we do not know. There could be a tendency for some to reason that it is not going to happen during my lifetime, so why get in a hurry to be ready? That could lead to failure to prepare. No doubt, it was this or similar reasoning that caused the apostle to admonish these Christians to live a holy life; to love each other; to be alert and self-controlled in order to be ready when the Lord returned (1 Thessalonians, chapters four and five). He contrasted Jesus' return to that of a thief who shows up at night or to labor pains that suddenly come to a pregnant woman. It is vital that we stay alert, ready and prepared so that his coming does not find us unprepared.

The following things will happen according to 1 Thessalonians 4:13-18.

- Jesus will come again. God will bring with Jesus those who have fallen asleep in him.
- The Lord will come down from heaven, and with a loud command, will first call out of the graves those who have died.
- We who are still living when the Lord returns will not precede (go before) those who have fallen asleep or are already dead.
- The living will be caught up together with them in the clouds to meet the Lord in the air.
- Both groups will, together, *be with the Lord forever*—not on the earth, but in heaven.

Chapter four ends with, "Therefore encourage each other with these words."

John, in the Book of Revelation, wrote:

> Look, he is coming with the clouds, and every eye will see him, even those who pierced him. The next verse states, "I am the Alpha and the Omega," says the Lord God, "who is and who was, and who is to come, the Almighty' (Revelation 1:7, 8).

No misunderstanding should exist regarding his coming or his reason for coming, since the apostle states that every eye will see him. Paul adds that those in Jesus will be caught up in the air to be with the Lord forever. Make no mistake: this world is not the Christian's permanent home! Remember how Jesus worded it: "I go to prepare a place for you.... I will come again, and receive you to Myself, that where I am, *there* you may be also" (John 14:2, 3, NASV).

Jesus has no plans to stay on this earth when he returns to receive us unto himself. Instead, he intends to take us where he has prepared a place suitable for a heavenly habitation.

The apostle's final admonition is: "But since we belong to the day, let us be self-controlled, putting on faith and love as a breastplate, and the hope of salvation as a helmet" (1 Thessalonians 5:8).

A few thoughts are needed to clarify and bring together the previous assertions.

Every human being, at birth, is provided an eternal nature. Jesus is describing this condition in Matthew, chapter 25. He uses the analogy of sheep and goats to make his point.

> When the Son of Man comes in his glory, and all the angels with him, he will sit on his throne in heavenly glory. All the nations will be gathered before him, and he will separate the people one from another as a shepherd separates the sheep from the goats. He will put the sheep on his right and the goats on his left (Matthew 25:31-33).

To those on his right, he says: "Come, you who are blessed by my Father; take your inheritance, the kingdom prepared for you since the creation of the world" (v. 34).

These people are referred to as "the righteous" and are the ones who have surrendered their lives to the Lord's will and carried out his instructions.

To the other group, he declares: "Depart from me, you who are cursed, into the eternal fire prepared for the devil and his angels" (v. 41).

Jesus gives a clear explanation for the separation of the two groups with this final proclamation. "Then they will go away to eternal punishment, but the righteous to eternal life" (v.46). It is not a case of their going into "punishment" and "life," but *"eternal punishment"* and *"eternal life,"* indicating that it continues forever.

The Reality of Eternal Life in Heaven

The reality of heaven is as certain as is the assurance of God our heavenly Father. Note the following Scriptures:

- "Heaven is my throne, and the earth is my footstool" (Isaiah 66:1; Acts 7:49).
- Jesus stated: "I have come down from heaven...to do the will of him who sent me" (John 6:38).
- When Jesus returned to heaven, two angels told the disciples, "This same Jesus, who has been taken from you into heaven, will come back in the same way you have seen him go into heaven'" (Acts 1:11).
- Jesus taught the disciples to begin prayer with these words: "'Our Father in heaven'" (Matthew 6:9). The Lord's permanent dwelling is
- in heaven. If we want to live in His presence forever, heaven must be our final goal.

The glory and Marvel of Heaven

Three people in the New Testament speak from experience regarding heaven—Stephen, the apostles Paul and John.

- Stephen was one of the seven chosen by the apostles to help care for the Grecian widows who were not receiving proper care (Acts 6:1-6). He was a man full of faith, the Holy Spirit and wisdom (6:3,5). Following his speech to the Sanhedrin, the people stoned him. As he was dying, he "looked up to heaven and saw the glory of God, and Jesus standing at the right hand of God" (7:55).
- Paul related a vision when he "was caught up to the third heaven" (2 Corinthians 12:2). He stated that he was unsure about whether it happened while he was in the body or out of

the body, but God knows. What is certain—he "was caught up into Paradise, and heard inexpressible words, which a man is not permitted to speak" (v. 4). Since he was not allowed to explain what he heard, we know little except that he could speak with certainty about Paradise (meaning, "garden of pleasure" or "garden of light"), and heaven's existence.

- In John's case, he was permitted to speak and write freely in the book of Revelation. In one of his visions he stated:

> After this I looked, and there before me was a door standing open in heaven. And the voice I had first heard speaking to me like a trumpet said, '"Come up here, and I will show you what must take place after this'" (Revelation 4:1). Later he adds, "'Then I looked and heard the voice of many angels.... In a loud voice they sang: 'Worthy is the Lamb, who was slain, to receive power and wealth and wisdom and strength and honor and glory and praise!' Then I heard every creature in heaven and on earth...singing: To him who sits on the throne and to the Lamb be praise and honor and glory and power, for ever and ever (5:11-13).

The apostle described a number of similar passages throughout the book of Revelation that he labeled from the beginning as a book of prophecy containing apocalyptic language. However, much of what he wrote is clear and easy to understand.

In the final two chapters, he described "a new heaven and a new earth" (21:1) and stated that the old order of things had passed away.

The Holy City, the new Jerusalem, is seen coming down out of heaven:

- ➢ This is *God's dwelling where He lives* with His people, and He will be their God (vv.1-4).

- There is no temple in the city "because the Lord God Almighty and the Lamb are its temple" (v.21).
- There is no need for the sun or moon to shine on it because "the *glory of God gives it light* and the *Lamb is its lamp*" (v. 23).
- The *gates will never be shut* because there will be *no night* there (v.25).
- Nothing *impure* will ever enter it—"only those whose names are written in the Lamb's book of life" (v. 27). Heaven is a holy place designed for people who are holy.
- *Death,* with its consequences, will not be present since no one dies (v. 4).
- No one *grows old* because *time* does not pass. It has ceased to exist (emphasis added).

John describes the gates of the city as being pure gold, like transparent glass; the walls are made of jasper; the foundations of the city wall are decorated with every kind of precious stone; and the twelve gates are made of twelve pearls. John is grasping for words when he writes that they are *like* transparent glass. His description, however, extends far beyond the vocabulary of the average person, exceeding the imagination.

The world in which we live is wonderful in many ways, but it is far from perfect. The things necessary to care for our physical bodies are available in abundance. The same is true of our emotional, psychological and spiritual needs if we are willing to put forth the effort to locate the source and absorb the benefits. This said: There is no certainty as to how long we will live in this imperfect environment. We are going to die, and that can happen at any age. No one can avoid death unless he/she is living when the Lord returns to gather his people to take them home to heaven.

The body in which this author resides is different in many ways from what it was in the prime of life. Now it houses a prosthetic knee; cartilage has been removed from the lower back; prostate cancer required surgery that called for an adjustment to function with satisfaction; glaucoma requires constant treatment to save the vision; the hearing is beginning to need assistance; not to include a host of other things that have kept me patched together and going at a reasonably good pace. Anyone who lives late into the senior years can expect similar things to happen.

On Friday evening, my wife and I were called to the hospital where we ministered to a brother in Christ who had been eating a steak and got choked. Fortunately, a member of the family was present who rushed him to the hospital. By the time we arrived, he was in the operating room waiting for the anesthesiologists to administer medication before the surgeon looked down his throat to locate the foreign object. As I looked around, I observed a room full of electronic equipment with a team of doctors and nurses monitoring everything hooked to the patient as they prepared for the surgery.

It suddenly occurred me, that everything in that room, including the hospital, the doctors and the nurses will *not be needed* where I am going because there is no sickness, pain, death or funerals in heaven.

Yesterday we were waiting to see the doctor in hopes of getting some relief for back pain when suddenly a man who does carpentry work walked in with a big corrugated nail protruding completely through his thumb. He had been using a nail gun that drives nails and accidentally got his thumb in the way. Just looking at the wound almost caused my wife to faint. When we left, he was still waiting for the surgeon to remove the nail. Accidents do happen in this world that are sometimes critical, and it will continue to be true until the end of this age.

Solomon summarized life's journey in a marvelous way as he finished writing Ecclesiastes.

> Remember your Creator in the days of your youth, before the days of trouble come and the years approach when you will say, "I find no pleasure in them"—before the sun and the light and the moon and the stars grow dark,...and the strong men stoop,

> when the grinders cease because they are few, and those looking through the windows grow dim;... Then man goes to his eternal home...and the dust returns to the ground it came from, and the spirit returns to God who gave it (Ecclesiastes 12:1, 2, 5,7).

Solomon wrote more in this chapter to describe our development from infancy to the senior years. He cautioned us to remember where we came from, (our Creator), why we are here, and to live so that when this journey is completed, we will pass to our eternal home.

The words of the spiritual song arranged by A. H. Howard, describe it beautifully:

"This world is not my home, I'm just a passing thru."

The apostle Paul put what is frequently called, *the finishing touch,* on it with these words:

> Now we know that if the earthly tent we live in is destroyed, we have a building from God, an eternal house in heaven, not built by human hands. (2 Corinthians 5:1).

A multitude of reasons exist for not wanting to live forever in this world.

At the top of the list are the following, to name a few:

- ✓ *Sin with its consequences*;
- ✓ sickness,
- ✓ pain,
- ✓ suffering,
- ✓ sorrow,
- ✓ grief,
- ✓ loneliness,

The end result, of course, is death—something that is not well understood. Death is the Lord's appointment, (Hebrews 9:27), but it need be nothing more than a transition from this physical life to *eternal life in heaven,* if we are trusting and serving Jesus.

Thus, our temporal, perishable, mortal body will be changed in an instant into one that is permanent, imperishable, immortal—equipped for eternal life in heaven. How any individual would pass up the opportunity to receive such a marvelous blessing is beyond comprehension. In heaven, God's glory and beauty will be observable everywhere. Anything touched by the artistic hand of our heavenly Father is certain to reflect the brilliance of His glory.

The words of Jesus from the Sermon on the Mount best serve to close out this section, followed with an appropriate song:

> Do not store up for yourselves treasures on earth, where moth and rust destroy, and where thieves break in and steal. But store up for yourselves treasures in heaven, where moth and rust do not destroy, and where thieves do not break in and steal. For where your treasure is, there your heart will be also (Matthew 6:19-21).

"Earth Holds No Treasure"

Words and Music by: Tillet S. Teddlie

Earth holds no treasures but perish with using,
However precious they be; Yet there's a country
to which I am going: Heaven holds all to me.

Heaven holds all to me, Brighter its glory will be;
Joy without measure, will be my treasure:
Heaven holds all to me.

These words of Jesus in Teddlie's song express my earnest intention once I have passed "through the valley of the shadow of death," as described by David in the 23rd Psalm. Indeed, heaven holds all to me! My desire and prayer is that you, the reader, will be able to say the same words, "When the Roll Is Called Up Yonder."

THE NEED FOR UNITY

It is my sincere hope that this review of the wonderful mission of Jesus will generate in you a desire to fulfill our Savior's prayer for unity among all believers. The gospel that is summarized above is simple and easy to understand; consequently, unity should not be an impossible objective to achieve.

Christ's prayer for unity. In John 17:20-23, Jesus prayed for unity among Christians down to the present day. He ended his prayer declaring three purposes for unity among those of us who believe and have obeyed the gospel.

First purpose: Our unity must stress the fact that Jesus is united with his Father:

> My prayer is not for them alone. I pray also for those who will believe in me through their message, *that all of them may be one*. Father, just as you are in me and I am in you. (v. 20, 21a, emphasis added)

Second purpose: His followers should reflect the unity that Jesus has with his Father because we have received a wonderful gift—the "glory" that God gave his Son.

> May they also be in us so that the world may believe that you have sent me. I have given them the *glory* that you gave me, *that they may be one as we are one*: I in them and you in me. (v. 21b, 22, emphasis added)

Third purpose: Our unity demonstrates to the world the presence of God's love for his Son—and for us.

> *May they be brought to complete unity* to let the world know that you sent me and have *loved them* even as you have loved me. (v. 23, emphasis added)

Therefore, the great need for unity among Christians exists today. The blessings of this unity should be greatly desired, as summarized in Jesus' prayer:

- ✓ We can come to know better the oneness of Jesus and God.
- ✓ We can receive a great blessing from our unity together: a measure of God's "glory." (Romans 8:30).
- ✓ We can experience and appreciate in greater measure the love that God has for us in sending his Son to this world in which we live.

This book is based on the belief that unity among believers is possible because Jesus prayed to God, his father, for it. UNITY IS POSSIBLE! It can be achieved by Christians being united on the simple gospel story described in the New Testament and quoted in this book. Our present-day religious divisions are caused by human additions to this simple story or by omitting parts of the gospel in our preaching and teaching.

This book ends by asking only two questions about unity that the reader should ponder and answer:

1. In light of Jesus' prayer for unity, why is the religious world so divided?
2. Since Jesus said, *"I will build my church,"* can we unite around the simple worship and doctrine that characterize the church that he built?

The characteristics of the church that Jesus built are not difficult to duplicate today because they were simple and easy to implement then. Note the following characteristics of the New Testament church that we studied in this book:

- ➢ *Becoming a Christian was simple.* Peter's reply to his audience's question on Pentecost—"Brothers, what must we do?"—was, Repent and be baptized...in the name of Jesus Christ for the forgiveness of your sins (Acts 2:38).
- ➢ *The worship of the New Testament church was not complicated.* It centered around the Lord's Supper and served to unite the followers every first day of the week (Sunday). (1Corinthians 16:2; 11:1-13; Acts 20:7. Can we be united with this type of worship today?
- ➢ *The worship in song was simple with Christians singing hymns of praise.* (1 Corinthians 14:6; Ephesians 5:19, 20). Can we be united with this type of singing in worship today?
- ➢ *Preaching was simple because it was based on the inspired Word of God,* not man's additions of creeds and traditions. (Hebrews 4:12 13). Is it possible to duplicate this characteristic of the New Testament church today? Remember, with God all things are possible.

Please consider these thoughts. We earnestly desire to join with you in answering the Lord's prayer for unity.

Summary

The last chapter explains why we must make heaven our eternal goal.

It describes what happens when we die—that physical death is the Lord's appointment (Hebrews

9:27), but need be nothing more than a transition from *physical life to eternal life* in heaven.

It briefly describes the beauty, glory and marvel of heaven.

It explains how there will be no sickness, suffering, pain, sorrow, grief, loneliness—no sin with its consequences—because there is no death there.

Conclusion

Every story to be complete must have an appropriate conclusion. This fact is true of human beings who are one of the central figures of this book. From the moment a child is born into this world, it becomes an eternal being designed to live forever; either with God in His eternal heaven or with Satan and his angels in eternal punishment (Matthew 25:31-46).

Two stages are involved for this to be complete. The first stage begins on earth and concludes when we die. The second stage begins following our death and resurrection to eternal life in heaven with God and His Spiritual family. This will continue forever.

Preparation for living with God and his people in heaven can only be accomplished while we are living on the earth. It involves seeking to do God's will as outlined in the Scriptures and accepting Jesus Christ as our Lord and Savior. This will equip us at death for our final journey to heaven.

In closing, the words of Jesus used to begin chapter one of this book have made a genuine impression on every thought included. *Do you remember?* To paraphrase: *There would be no benefit in gaining the entire world and losing our soul.* (Matthew 16:26). Its value exceeds everything else.

Surely you must be moved with the desire to accept God's marvelous gift of eternal life in heaven made possible through Jesus Christ. Heaven is real! God, Christ, the Holy Spirit and the best people who have ever lived will be there. Let us live so as to be included in that glorious family!

Endnotes

Chapter One
Mission of Jesus Christ

1 The word "man"—translated from the Greek word *anthropos*— is a generic term that can apply to both male and female. To render it as "a person" is acceptable.

Chapter Five
Miracles Performed by Jesus

1 **The Random House Dictionary of the English Language:** Jess Stern, Editor in Chief, Laurence Urdang, Managing Editor: (Random House/ New York,1973) 904.

Chapter Eight
Celebration of Pentecost

1 Henry E. Dosker, *The International Standard Bible Encyclopaedia*, Volume IV, 2318.

2 *A Greek – English Lexicon of the New Testament; Translated Revised and Enlarged by Joseph Henry Thayer*, Fourth Edition, Edinburgh T & T Clark, 38 George Street,1953) 82.

3 Fredrick William Danker, *A Greek-English Lexicon of The New Testament And Other Early Christian Literature*. Third Edition, (Chicago and London): The University of Chicago Press, 2000) 809.

4 Danker, 534.

Chapter Nine
Unity and the Church

1 (J. C. Lambert, *The International Standard Bible Encyclopaedia*. Vol. 111, 1952) 651.

Chapter Twelve
Appeal for Unity

1 (William Hendricksen, *New Testament Commentary, Ephesians:* Grand Rapids, Baker Book House, 1967) 187.

Bibliography

Primary Sources:

Nestle, Erwin, et Aland, Kurt; NOVUM TESTAMENTUM GRAECE: New York, Privileg. Wurtt, Bibelanstalt Stuttgart. 1957.

Danker, Frederick William; *A Greek-English Lexicon of the New Testament and Other Early Christian Literature*: Third Edition, Chicago and London, The University of Chicago Press, 2000.

Thayer, Joseph Henry; *A Greek English Lexicon of the New Testament, Fourth Edition: (Edinburg T & T Clark, 38 George Street) 1953.*

New American Standard Bible: La Habra, Calif., The Lockman Foundation, Moody Press; 1973.

New International Version: International Bible Society; Zondervan Bible Publishers, 1973, 1978, 1984.

Authorized King James Version: Cleveland, Ohio, The World Publishing Company, 1611.

Secondary Sources:

Hendricksen, William: *New Testament Commentary, Ephesians*: Grand Rapids, Baker Book House; 1967.

Orr, James, General Editor, *The International Standard Bible Encyclopedia;* Vol. 111, William B. Eerdmans Publishing Co., Grand Rapids, Mich.,1952.

Orr, James, General Editor,*The International Standard Bible Encyclopaedia;* Vol. IV, William B. Eerdmans Publishing Co., Grand Rapids, Mich., 1952

Printed in the United States
By Bookmasters